SELECTED WRITINGS

SIR THOMAS BROWNE was born in 1605, the son of a merchant, and was educated at Winchester School and Oxford University. He studied medicine in the leading European medical schools, becoming a Doctor of Medicine at Leiden in 1633, returning to England to practise medicine for four years in Oxfordshire, during which time he probably wrote *Religio Medici*. In 1637 he qualified as a Doctor of Medicine at Oxford and established his medical practice in Norwich, where he lived for the rest of his life. He married in 1641, and in 1642, the year in which the English Civil War broke out, his first child was born. *Religio Medici* was published in the same year. Although Norwich was a centre of Puritan sympathy, Browne appears to have been little involved in the politics of the day, and continued to write and practise medicine. *Pseudodoxia Epidemica* was first published in 1650 and *Urn Burial* in 1658. In 1671 Browne was knighted by Charles II during a visit to Norwich. Sir Thomas Browne died in 1682.

CLAIRE PRESTON is Fellow and Director of Studies in English, Sidney Sussex College, Cambridge, UK. She has a particular interest in Renaissance literature and has published on Shakespeare and Philip Sydney, as well as works on modern American literature.

Fyfield*Books* aim to make available some of the great classics of British and European literature in clear, affordable formats, and to restore often neglected writers to their place in literary tradition.

Fyfield*Books* take their name from the Fyfield elm in Matthew Arnold's 'Scholar Gypsy' and 'Thyrsis'. The tree stood not far from the village where the series was originally devised in 1971.

> *Roam on! The light we sought is shining still.*
> *Dost thou ask proof? Our tree yet crowns the hill,*
> *Our Scholar travels yet the loved hill-side*

from 'Thyrsis'

SIR THOMAS BROWNE

Selected Writings

Edited with an introduction by
CLAIRE PRESTON

Fyfield*Books*

CARCANET

First published in Great Britain in 1995 by
Carcanet Press Limited
Alliance House
Cross Street
Manchester M2 7AQ
This impression 2003

A CIP catalogue record for this book is available from the British Library
ISBN 1 85754 690 3

The publisher acknowledges financial assistance from
the Arts Council of England

Printed and bound in England by SRP Ltd, Exeter

CONTENTS

Contents

¶Browne sends his autobiography to John Aubrey

14 March 1672/3

...I was born in St Michael's Cheap in London, went to school at Winchester College, then went to Oxford, spent some years in foreign parts, was admitted to be a *Socius Honorarius*[1] of the College of Physicians in London, Knighted September, 1671, when the King, Queen and Court came to Norwich. Writ *Religio Medici* in English, which was since translated into Latin, French, Italian, High and Low Dutch.[2]

    Pseudodoxia Epidemica, or Enquiries into Common and Vulgar Errors translated into Dutch four or five years ago.

    Hydriotaphia,or Urn Buriall.

    Hortus Cyri, or de Quincunce.

Have some miscellaneous tracts which may be published....

Letters 376

1] honorary fellow   2] German, and Dutch or Flemish

INTRODUCTION: 'JANUS IN THE FIELD OF KNOWLEDGE'

In 1605, the year of Browne's birth, Francis Bacon published *The Advancement of Learning*, the great call to engage in an experimental and pragmatic science. The call was already being answered in Europe, but the so-called Experimental Philosophy was not to receive the imprimatur of the establishment in England until 1662, the year in which Charles II granted his charter to the fledgling Royal Society. Bacon, half a century before, had imagined just such an institution, but the turmoils of civil unrest and disruption probably prevented official acknowledgement of the new science. Nevertheless, men of learning had been conducting their own experiments and observations and meeting, sometimes, in small groups in London or Oxford, to discuss their findings.

Between *The Advancement of Learning* and the foundation of the Royal Society, Browne was educated and produced all his major work. He was, in other words, in his intellectual prime during the watershed years before the official recognition of what we must call 'modern', empirical science. This was the twilight of classical authorities such as Aristotle, Galen, and Pliny; this was the period in which an intellectual sceptic like Browne might ply the waters of learning and help to rewrite the navigational charts by which the dawning experimental age would steer its course.

Thomas Browne (1605-82) lived through one of the most invigorating, calamitous, and astonishing of English centuries. Civil insurrection, regicide, Interregnum, colonization, naval warfare, scientific revolution, sectarianism, millenarianism: in short, a nation and a culture in the uncomfortable transition from Renaissance to Enlightenment. Unlike his greatest literary contemporaries – Marvell and Milton – Thomas Browne kept his distance from most of this upheaval. Although *Religio Medici* was undoubtedly a *succès d'estime* and brought, as well, the excoriations of the radical Protestants and the

Anglo-Catholics upon him, he averred he could not 'conceive why a difference of opinion should divide an affection; for controversies, disputes, and argumentations, both in philosophy and in divinity ... do not infringe the laws of charity' (*RM* II.3).

He was not a polemicist, a propagandist, an evangelist, or an allegorist, abstentions that at first seem to marginalize him in this era of controversies. He was a meditative observer and searcher-out of truth, whose contemplations of his maker constitute, as he says, 'the antiquary's truest object'. To investigate the world and its accidents is to glorify God and his purposes; they 'most powerfully magnify Him... who... from experiments and undeniable effects enforce the wonder of [their] Maker' (*PE* II.iii). Everything Browne wrote, scientific and philosophical, was a work of devotion.

In many respects, therefore, Browne's biography reads like a series of omissions. He made little direct contribution to the scientific discussion of his day by remaining hidden away (relatively speaking) in Norwich; he was not a member of the Royal Society (a fact which has needlessly puzzled many scholars), being too far away to participate; he apparently shunned publicity, if we are to believe his excuses for the surreptitious publication of *Religio Medici*, yet was esteemed all over Europe both for this work and for the magisterial *Pseudodoxia Epidemica*; he corresponded, as we would expect, with a selection of the outstanding scientists and writers of his generation. He *was* an Honorary Fellow of the Royal College of Physicians, as he is careful to point out in his terse autobiographical statement to John Aubrey, but almost carelessly he reels off the list of his printed works and mistakes a fact or two about them. It was left to his son, Edward, to garner the sort of social prominence his father seems to have avoided. The fashionable doctor to the king, member of the Royal Society and of the Royal College (as well as its president), the travelling *raporteur* whose observations of foreign countries were commissioned and eagerly expected by the learned circles in London, the physician who studied how to make a thousand pounds a year, and later in life, made good, bought himself a country seat – this was the son Edward, not the far more talented father Thomas.

Born the son of a well-to-do merchant, Browne was sent first to Winchester and then to Oxford, where by 1629 he was MA. The next four years were spent in medical studies at Montpellier, Padua, and Leiden, the latter two being the foremost institutions at this time for such an education. He became Doctor of Medicine at Leiden in 1633; and after a further four years of apprentice practice in Oxfordshire, during which time he probably wrote *Religio Medici*, he was incorporated Doctor of Medicine at Oxford.

The education of Thomas Browne was of the most liberal kind. Winchester and Oxford offered him a traditional, ample grounding in classical learning: grammar, logic, rhetoric, music, astronomy, arithmetic, and geometry were the core of the BA, with natural and moral philosophy and metaphysics to follow in the MA. This course of study was at least partially overseen by the flamboyant latitudinarian Thomas Lushington, whose broad views may well have influenced Browne's own. Science, or 'natural philosophy', at Oxford was in a primitive state, and like many intending doctors Browne continued his education on the Continent where he was more likely to meet with innovation. In Montpellier he would have heard the anatomy and botany lectures of Rondelet and Rivière; at Padua, where Vesalius and Fabricius had established practical anatomy and surgery as foundations of the medical course, and where William Harvey, the discoverer of blood circulation, had qualified as a doctor, Browne would no doubt have followed the trial then in progress of the former Paduan professor Galileo, a signal case which pitted received classical and Biblical information against empirical observation. At the new university of Leiden (est. 1575) the (then) peculiar combination of practical training (in the anatomy theatre, the physic garden, and the hospital ward) and reverence for standard Greek, Latin, and Arabic authorities (Hippocrates, Galen and Avicenna) was another picture in small of the competing methodologies of the bookish Scholastic heritage and the new, clinical science, a competition which exercised and invigorated natural philosophy throughout the century. It is a picture, also, of Browne himself, who could on one hand declare 'prostration unto Antiquity a powerful enemy unto knowledge', and on the other, that 'Galen and Hippocrates must be had as fathers and fountains of the faculty'.

Although he described his life as miraculous and fabulous, this is a statement we must, unlike Dr Johnson, read as tropically, as metaphorically as he could wish. The correspondent of several leading men of letters and science but not himself an innovator; a reluctant and accidental recipient of a knighthood on the occasion of a royal visit; a man who died in his bed on his birthday, full of years – the life of Sir Thomas Browne was hardly miraculous; in the strict historical sense, it was a life on the periphery.

Thomas Browne's literary contribution, was, on the other hand, central and distinctive. The range and variety of his work is (to use an

analogy which he might, perhaps, have appreciated) like an archaeological core-sample of the varied strata of seventeenth century intellectual concerns. *Religio Medici* is manifesto of personal articles of
faith and their theological consequences; *Pseudodoxia Epidemica* is a
huge catalogue of ancient and modern errors corrected (together with
the extraordinary familiarity with the vast edifice of western learning
such a project entails); *The Garden of Cyrus* is a graceful arabesque of
an essay on numerology in nature, half playful, half pedantic;
*Hydriotaphia: Urn-Burial, or, A Brief Discourse of the Sepulchral Urns
Lately Found in Norfolk* is a majestic and sonorous account of burial
rites through the ages, and their intimations of mortality; and his notebooks, tracts, and letters are packed with observations and *quaeres* on
topics ranging from magnetism, ostriches, geography, echoes, dreams,
plant and animal taxonomy, and fossils, to whispering chambers,
mummies, home remedies, local politics, ladies' dress, and garlands;
even these fugitive pieces are a monument to his relentless curiosity.

Although he couches it in the resonant periods of his great meditative, metaphysical works, Browne values knowledge, above all, for its
utility. As a practising doctor he could hardly do otherwise; but also as
a practising Christian, scientist, and naturalist, the pursuit of knowledge expurgated error – the heritage and embodiment of Satan – and
offered proximity to God's unsearchable purposes in the Creation.
The arena of Browne's personal fascinations and enthusiasms displays
a polymath of immense and concentrated interests, informed and at
home, like his correspondents Robert Boyle, William Dugdale, Elias
Ashmole, Robert Cotton and John Evelyn, in virtually every branch of
human enquiry. To read Sir Thomas Browne is to open a window on
the seventeenth century.

Standing like Janus in the field of knowledge, looking back at ancient authority and honouring it, but looking forward to the implica-
tions of contemporary developments in physics, chemistry, anatomy,
astronomy, embryology, mechanics, archaeology, etymology, and
ethnology, Browne is in many ways an exemplary seventeenth-century
figure. While completing his medical apprenticeship in Oxfordshire
between 1633 and 1637, he wrote his first and most remarkable work,
Religio Medici. Although this extraordinary *summa* of his philosophy
and faith was complete when he was scarcely thirty years old, it estab-
lishes in clear strokes the character and predilections of his later works.
The first version of the essay was, he claimed, secretly and without his
permission conveyed to a printer who brought out an anonymous
edition in 1642, and then another in the same year when sales proved

brisk. When the Earl of Dorset recommended the pirated book to Sir Kenelm Digby late in the year, that picturesque dilettante, by his own account at least, stayed up all night to read it and to pen his *Observations upon Religio Medici*. These were published a few months later, and the subsequent publicity forced Browne to bring out an authorized edition of *Religio* to which his name was attached. The book attracted considerable attention both in England and on the Continent, where it was translated into several languages and even found its way onto the recommended list of Emperor Rudolph's librarian. It established Browne as a stylist of rare power and as a belletrist of profound erudition. *Religio Medici* is a self-portrait of 'that great and true Amphibium', equally at home in contemplations of the earthly and the divine, his style not so much sermonic as a blend of classical and Biblical rhythms in which his subject is unfolded and ramified in what Robin Robbins has described as a 'non-dialectical' fashion of thought.

The year 1642 was momentous in other ways, politically and personally. The Civil War began, and Browne's first child was born. It is clear that Browne's purpose in issuing a corrected and revised version of *Religio Medici* was to protect himself from imputations of a political partisanship which might have got him in trouble at this very unstable moment. But other than an allusion to anti-royalist pamphlets at the beginning, and the famous remark that coition 'is the foolishest act a wise man commits in all his life' (*RM* II.9), nothing in the essay itself gives direct indication of its historical or biographical provenance. In 1637 Browne had settled in Norwich (then the second metropolis of England), and established his medical practice. In 1641 he married Dorothy Mileham. In the months and years following the publication of *Religio Medici*, Charles I abandoned London and joined battle with the Parliamentary forces, the New Model Army was established, Archbishop Laud was impeached and executed, the episcopacy was abolished, and Oliver Cromwell won the first of his important battles against the king. During this time Browne wrote and published the first version of *Pseudodoxia Epidemica*, a work perhaps obliquely determined by current events in its prevailing doubts about adherence to established authority, but otherwise unconcerned with politics and governments. Browne was a professed Royalist, or perhaps more accurately, a conservative traditionalist whose views were characteristic of many of the educated gentry. His toleration, especially in matters of religion, brought upon him the contumely of radical Puritans such as Alexander Ross, but was equally dangerous to the High Church element which was actively engaged in suppressing alternative beliefs and practices. Browne's views cut both ways: he is at once unwilling to be intimidated either by the literal-mindedness of sectarian theology or the political authoritarianism of the established church. Books V and VII of *Pseudodoxia Epidemica* offer to explode specific errors, ancient and modern, in the interpretation of Scripture, errors dear to each side in the political dispute.

Although Norwich was a centre of Puritan sympathy, its Cathedral mutilated by parliamentary troops in 1641, it is difficult to say what part Browne took in the the decades of the Civil War and the Interregnum. They appear to have passed uneventfully; but as physician to Joseph Hall, the Royalist Bishop of Norwich who had been turned out of his residence by the Parliamentarians, and as signatory of two separate Royalist pamphlets, he cannot have been wholly uninvolved. Since he preserved almost none of his correspondence before 1660, a sense of seclusion from events may be merely the impression given by his published works. Unless his tolerant remarks in *Religio Medici* be construed as clearly Anglican, he left no political opinions.

The tenor of the times produced so much overtly polemical writing that we have come almost to expect contention as a feature of mid-seventeenth century literature. But as much historical research continues to remind us, the upheavals of the Civil War and the antecedent period did not, perhaps, engulf the whole nation so irresistibly as we are inclined to believe. It was quite possible for the politically sensitive intellectual to have opinions and sympathies in the conflict which did not necessarily inform or even surface in his work. Besides, Browne's daily experiences as a provincial doctor must have pressed much more vigorously in a period when life expectancy was still low, and most common afflictions were incurable or fatal. He remarks, 'I... have examined the parts of man, and know upon what tender filaments that fabric hangs' (*RM* I.44). The main events of the Civil War and the Interregnum may have seemed remote from the daily round of life and death. That *Pseudodoxia* was substantially enlarged and revised in four further editions published between 1650 and 1672 suggests relative leisure: and the elegant exercises of *Urn-Burial* and *The Garden of Cyrus* were produced and published by 1658.

Browne's reputation in English letters has always been high without being familiar. He is the sort of writer who, in the face of competition from Shakespeare, Jonson, Bacon, Burton, and the Jacobean and Caroline poets in the first half of the century, and from Hobbes, Marvell, and above all Milton in the second half, is more known about than known. This is unfortunate, but quite reasonable. For one thing,

INTRODUCTION 7

his *oeuvre* is large, and with few exceptions comprehends works too long or too concentrated to be digested readily or comfortably. Secondly, like Burton, Browne is among the most recondite of writers: when not proposing himself as his subject (a topic quite remote enough), his enthusiasms are specialist, learned, antiquarian, obscure. His style, often meditative in the most striking ways, is nevertheless labyrinthine and baroque: the texture of his thought is studded with allusion, reference, understatement, and quotation in ancient languages. In short, Browne is uncompromising and difficult, even to the ear tempered by mid-seventeenth century rhythms; it requires a number of readings to make sense of much he says; and even then, the range of reference can seem fearsome and prohibitive.

The purpose of this edition is both investigative and polemical. Like the archaeological core-sample, it aims to offer a selection of Browne's work which will allow the new reader to get an idea of his range and style without being overwhelmed by it, but it is also designed to set off Browne's startling, if sometimes hidden, merit. Even Browne's most accessible writings – *Religio Medici, Urn-Burial, The Garden of Cyrus* and occasionally the more prepossessing chapters from *Pseudodoxia Epidemica* – are a rich and concentrated mixture. Although these are unquestionably his major works, they are difficult to read from end to end without context or explanation; and their domination of his canon occludes his other more minor but no less characteristic pieces.

After his visit to Dr Browne of Norwich in 1671, John Evelyn, the famous gossip and diarist, noted that the house was 'a paradise and cabinet of rarities…'. I have tried to imitate that cabinet in this choice of Browne's work. In the following pages selections from major and minor writings are arranged in thematic sections which recognize Browne's principal concerns and the full variety of their expression: I hope that the more familiar sonorities of *Urn-Burial* and *Religio Medici* will be usefully highlighted by, for example, Browne's Polonian advice to his son Tom in France, his puzzling over the nomenclature of coastal birds with Christopher Merrett, and his plangent arithmetic reckoning the cost of a large family. The reader will find relatively more of Browne's purely scientific writing than is usual, and that with a care to introduce a few neglected areas of writing such as his letters on ornithology and some of the fascinating *Miscellany Tracts*; and somewhat less of the readily available *Religio Medici*, his masterpiece. One work, *Urn-Burial*, is reproduced entire because it is in many ways most characteristic of Browne.

The texture of Browne's prose would be irrecoverable if the constant reference to his sources were omitted, even though his recondite allusions make what now seem insuperable barriers for the modern reader. In fact, such references are rarely central to his argument, and to gloss each one would distract from the rhythm of his thought; but to assist the curious, an index of sources and other proper names has been supplied at the end of the volume. Browne was also a vigorous neologist: 'medical', 'literary', 'electricity', 'precarious', 'hallucination', and 'antediluvian' are but a few of his innovations, and show how needy seventeenth-century investigative writing was of new terms. Such instances have been noted in the glosses.

No serious modern reader or editor of Browne can but acknowledge with relief the work of previous scholars in this century, without which the present task would have been virtually impossible. Sir Geoffrey Keynes's revised edition of Browne's *Works* (Chicago, 1964) forms the basis of the present edition, as does Robin Robbins's invaluable annotated *Pseudodoxia Epidemica* (Oxford, 1981). In addition, the selected editions of Browne by L.C. Martin (Oxford, 1964), C.A. Patrides (Harmondsworth, 1977), and Robin Robbins (Oxford, 1982) have been very useful. I am responsible for all departures from their judgements, and for any errors in my own.

I wish also to thank the following libraries for their patience and assistance: the Robert Taylor Collection of the Firestone Library, Princeton University; Cambridge University Library, the Muniments Room of Sidney Sussex College, the library of Pembroke College, Cambridge; the Hawthorne-Longfellow Library, Bowdoin College, Maine; and the Bodleian Library. Many people have answered many questions: these were James Basker, Robert Boutilier, Susan Brigden, John Corner, Nick Davies, Adrian Friday, Roy Gibson, Laura Gilbert, Gabriel Horn, Lynn Hulse, Kevin Jackson, Judith Maltby, Jeremy Maule, Joseph Merrill, Christopher Page, Christopher Parrish, Richard Preston, Nicholas Rogers, Lenaye Siegel, Helen Taylor, and Ian Wallis. I wish to record my gratitude to the Master and Fellows of Sidney Sussex College, Cambridge, for granting the sabbatical leave during part of which this work was completed.

A NOTE ON THE TEXT

The text of this edition is based on Sir Geoffrey Keynes's revised second edition of Browne's works (Chicago, 1964). Capitalization, punctuation, and spelling have been modernized (the latter only as far as is consistent with Browne's rhythm and pronunciation). A few of Browne's own explanatory glosses and marginalia have been retained; these are indicated by inverted commas. Passages have been reproduced whole whenever possible; some cuts, however, have been made, and these are indicated by four dots.

All page references in the following abbreviations refer to *The Complete Works of Sir Thomas Browne* ed. Geoffrey Keynes, second revised edition (Chicago, 1964):

* A word or meaning first recorded as Browne's in OED

** A word or usage not recorded in OED

RM: *Religio Medici*; Roman and Arabic numerals refer to book and section numbers

UB: *Urn-Burial*; Roman numerals refer to section numbers

GC: *The Garden of Cyrus*; Roman and Arabic numerals refer to chapter and page numbers

PE: *Pseudodoxia Epidemica*; upper and lower case Roman, and Arabic numerals refer to book, chapter, and page numbers

CP: *Commonplace Books*; page numbers are given

LF: *Letter to a Friend*; page numbers are given

Letters: page numbers are given

Notes: *Notebooks*; page numbers are given

Tracts: *Miscellany Tracts*; Roman and Arabic numbers refer to tract and page numbers

CM: *Christian Morals*; Roman and Arabic numbers refer to section and page numbers

FURTHER READING

Morris Croll, 'The Baroque Style in Prose' in *Studies in Philology in Honour of Frederick Klaeber*, ed. K. Malone and M.B. Ruud (1929)

Stanley Fish, 'The Bad Physician: The Case of Sir Thomas Browne' in *Self-Consuming Artifacts: The Experience of Seventeenth Century Literature* (1972)

S.K. Heninger, *Touches of Sweet Harmony: Pythagorean Cosmology and Renaissance Poetics* (1974)

Michael Hunter, *Science and Society in Restoration England* (1981)

Arnaldo Momigliano, 'Ancient History and the Antiquarian' in *Studies in Historiography* (1966)

C.A. Patrides, ed., *Approaches to Sir Thomas Browne: The Ann Arbor Tercentenary Lectures and Essays* (1982)

Stuart Piggott, *Ruins in a Landscape: Essays in Antiquarianism* (1976)

C.E. Preston, '"Unriddling the World": Sir Thomas Browne and the Doctrine of Signatures' *Critical Survey* 5, no. 2 (1993)

Alexander Ross, *Medicus Medicatus* (1645)

Thomas Sprat, *The History of the Royal Society of London* (1667)

Frank J. Warnke, 'A Hook for Amphibium: Some Reflections on Fish' in *Approaches to Sir Thomas Browne*, ed. C.A. Patrides

Austin Warren, 'The Styles of Sir Thomas Browne' in *Seventeenth Century Prose*, ed Stanley Fish (1971)

Margaret Wiley, *The Subtle Knot* (1952)

Basil Willey, *The Seventeenth Century Background* (1955)

James N. Wise, *Sir Thomas Browne's Religio Medici and Two Seventeenth Century Critics* (1973)

I. RELIGION

¶ *Religio Medici*:[1]
To the Reader

Certainly that man were greedy of life, who should desire to live when all the world were at an end; and he must needs be very impatient, who would repine at death in the society of all things that suffer under it. Had not almost every man suffered by the press, or were not the tyranny thereof become universal, I had not wanted reason for complaint: but in times wherein I have lived to behold the highest perversion of that excellent invention[2] – the name of his Majesty defamed, the honour of Parliament depraved, the writings of both depravedly, anticipatively, counterfeitly imprinted – complaints may seem ridiculous in private persons, and men of my condition may be as incapable of affronts, as hopeless of their reparations. And truly, had not the duty I owe unto the importunity of friends and the allegiance I must ever acknowledge unto truth prevailed with me, the inactivity of my disposition might have made these sufferings continual, and time, that brings other things to light, should have satisfied me in the remedy of its oblivion. But because things evidently false are not only printed, but many things of truth most falsely set forth, in this latter I could not but think myself engaged: for though we have no power to redress the former, yet in the other the reparation being within ourselves, I have at present represented unto the world a full and intended copy of that piece which was most imperfectly and surreptitiously published before.[3]

This, I confess, about seven years past, with some others of affinity thereto, for my private exercise and satisfaction I had at leisurable hours composed; which being communicated unto one, it became common unto many, and was by transcription successively corrupted

1] *Religio Medici* 'a doctor's religion'   2] i.e. printing   3] two unauthorized editions of *RM* appeared in 1642; the 1643 edition (reproduced here) was modified and approved for publication by Browne

until it arrived in a most depraved copy at the press. He that shall peruse that work, and shall take notice of sundry particularities and personal expressions therein, will easily discern the intention was not public; and being a private exercise directed to myself, what is delivered therein was rather a memorial unto me than an example or rule unto any other; and therefore if there be any singularity therein correspondent unto the private conceptions of any man, it doth not advantage them; or if dissentaneous[4] thereunto, it no way overthrows them. It was penned in such a place and with such disadvantage, that (I protest) from the first setting of pen unto paper I had not the assistance of any good book whereby to promote my invention or relieve my memory; and therefore there might be many real lapses therein which others might take notice of, and more that I suspected myself. It was set down many years past, and was the sense of my conceptions at that time, not an immutable law unto my advancing judgement at all times, and therefore there might be many things therein plausible unto my past apprehension which are not agreeable unto my present self. There are many things delivered rhetorically, many expressions therein merely tropical[5] and as they best illustrate my intention; and therefore also there are many things to be taken in a soft and flexible sense, and not to be called unto the rigid test of reason. Lastly, all that is contained therein is in submission unto maturer discernments and, as I have declared, shall no further father them than the best and learned judgements shall authorise them; under favour of which considerations I have made its secrecy public and committed the truth thereof to every ingenuous[6] reader.

RM 'To the Reader'

¶ Reason and belief

As for those wingy mysteries in divinity and airy subtleties in religion which have unhinged the brains of better heads, they never stretched the *pia mater* of mine; methinks there be not impossibilities enough in religion for an active faith; the deepest mysteries ours contains have not only been illustrated, but maintained by syllogism and the rule of reason: I love to lose myself in a mystery, to pursue my reason to an *o altitudo*.[1] 'Tis my solitary recreation to pose my apprehension with

4] disagreeing   5] figurative; relating to tropes   6] generous, straightforward

1] '*O the depth* of riches both of the wisdom and knowledge of God! how unsearchable are his judgements, and his ways past finding out!' (Romans 11:33)

those involved enigmas and riddles of the Trinity, with incarnation and resurrection. I can answer all the objections of Satan, and my rebellious reason, with that odd resolution I learned of Tertullian, *Certum est quia impossibile est.*[2] I desire to exercise my faith in the difficultest points, for to credit ordinary and visible objects is not faith, but persuasion.[3] Some believe the better for seeing Christ his sepulture, and when they have seen the Red Sea, doubt not of the miracle. Now contrarily, I bless myself and am thankful that I lived not in the days of miracles, that I never saw Christ nor his disciples; I would not have been one of the Israelites that passed the Red Sea, nor one of Christ's patients, on whom he wrought his wonders; then had my faith been thrust upon me, nor should I enjoy that greater blessing pronounced to all that believe and saw not. 'Tis an easy and necessary belief to credit what our eye and sense hath examined: I believe he was dead, and buried, and rose again, and desire to see him in his glory, rather than to contemplate him in his cenotaph, or sepulchre. Nor is this much to believe: as we have reason, we owe this faith unto history: they only had the advantage of a bold and noble faith; who lived before his coming, who upon obscure prophecies and mystical types[4] could raise a belief, and expect apparent impossibilities.

RM I.9

¶Analogy and belief

'Tis true, there is an edge in all firm belief, and with an easy metaphor we may say 'the sword of faith'; but in these obscurities I rather use it in the adjunct the Apostle[1] gives it: a buckler;[2] under which I perceive a wary combatant may lie invulnerable. Since I was of understanding to know we know nothing, my reason hath been more pliable to the will of faith; I am now content to understand a mystery without a rigid definition in an easy and Platonic description.[3] That allegorical description of Hermes[4] pleaseth me beyond all the metaphysical definitions of the divines; where I cannot satisfy my reason, I love to

2] 'It is certain because it is impossible.'   3] belief through empirical proof
4] Old Testament prefigurations of New Testament events

1] Paul to the Ephesians 6:16   2] shield   3] one which acknowledges its unsearchability in a mystical rather than a precise expression   4] 'God is a sphere whose centre is everywhere, whose circumference is nowhere': an expression of Hermetic (i.e. mystical, Neoplatonic) philosophy

humour my fancy; I had as leif you tell me that *anima est angelus hominis, est corpus Dei*, as *Entelechia*;[5] *Lux est umbra Dei*, as *actus perspicui*.[6] Where there is an obscurity too deep for our reason, 'tis good to sit down with a description, periphrasis, or adumbration; for by acquainting our reason how unable it is to display the visible and obvious effects of nature, it becomes more humble and submissive unto the subtleties of faith: and thus I teach my haggard[7] and unreclaimed reason to stoop unto the lure of faith. I believe there was already a tree whose fruit our unhappy parents tasted, though in the same chapter, where God forbids it, 'tis positively said, the plants of the field were not yet grown, for God had not caused it to rain upon the earth. I believe that the serpent (if we shall literally understand it), from his proper form and figure, made his motion on his belly before the curse. I find the trial of the pucellage and virginity of women, which God ordained the Jews,[8] is very fallible. Experience and history inform me that not only many particular women, but likewise whole nations have escaped the curse of childbed, which God seems to pronounce upon the whole sex;[9] yet do I believe that all this is true, which indeed my reason would persuade me to be false; and this, I think, is no vulgar part of faith, to believe a thing not only above, but contrary to reason, and against the argument of our proper senses.

RM I.10

¶ The darkened glass

'Beware of philosophy'[1] is a precept not to be received in too large a sense; for in this mass of nature there is a set of things that carry in their front, though not in capital letters, yet in stenography and short characters,[2] something of divinity, which to wiser reasons serve as luminaries in the abyss of knowledge, and to judicious beliefs, as scales and roundels[3] to mount the pinnacles and highest pieces of divinity. The severe Schools[4] shall never laugh me out of the philosophy of Hermes, that this visible world is but a picture of the invisible, wherein, as in a portrait, things are not truly, but in equivocal shapes, and as they counterfeit some more real substance in that invisible fabric.

RM I.12

5] 'The soul is the angel of man, is the body of God,' as 'essence'
6] 'Light is the shadow of God', as 'actual transparency'.   7] wild (hawking term)   8] Deuteronomy 22:13-21   9] Genesis 3:16

1] Colossians 2:8   2] signatures   3] ladders and rungs   4] the anti-Hermetic Scholastic philosophers

¶ Pieces of wonder

Natura nihil agit frustra[1] is the only indisputable axiom in philosophy; there are no grotesques in nature, nor anything framed to fill up
empty cantons and unnecessary spaces; in the most imperfect creatures, and such as were not preserved in the Ark, but having their seeds
and principles in the womb of nature, are everywhere where the power
of the sun is; in these is the wisdom of his hand discovered; out of this
rank Solomon chose the object of his admiration;[2] indeed what reason
may not go to school to the wisdom of bees, ants, and spiders? What
wise hand teacheth them to do what reason cannot teach us? Ruder
heads stand amazed at those prodigious pieces of nature, whales, elephants, dromedaries, and camels; these I confess, are the colossus and
majestic pieces of her hand; but in these narrow engines[3] there is more
curious mathematics, and the civility of these little citizens more neatly
sets forth the wisdom of their maker. Who admires not Regiomontanus his fly beyond his eagle,[4] or wonders not more at the operation of two souls in those little bodies, than but one in the trunk of a
cedar?[5] I could never content my contemplation with those general
pieces of wonder, the flux and reflux of the sea, the increase of the
Nile, the conversion of the needle to the north; and have studied to
match and parallel those in the more obvious and neglected pieces of
nature, which without further travel I can do in the cosmography of
myself. We carry with us the wonders we seek without us: there is all
Africa and her prodigies in us; we are that bold and adventurous piece
of nature which he that studies wisely learns, in a compendium, what
others labour at in a divided piece and endless volume.

RM I.15

¶ The world as text

Thus, there are two books from whence I collect my divinity: besides
that written one of God, another of his servant nature, that universal

1] 'Nature does nothing without purpose' (Aristotle)   2] Proverbs 6:6-8: 'the
ant...having no guide, overseer, or ruler, provideth her meat in the summer, and
gathereth her food in the harvest'; 30:28: 'The spider taketh hold with her hands,
and is in kings' palaces.'   3] clever devices   4] the mechanical fly and eagle,
said to be capable of flight, built by the fifteenth-century inventor Johan Muller of
Königsberg   5] Aristotle proposed three souls in mankind (rational, sensitive and
vegetative), of which animals were thought to have last two, and plants only the last

and public manuscript that lies expansed unto the eyes of all; those that never saw him in the one, have discovered him in the other. This was the scripture and theology of the heathens. The natural motion of the sun made them more admire him than its supernatural station[1] did the children of Israel; the ordinary effects of nature wrought more admiration in them than in the other all his miracles; surely the heathens knew better how to join and read these mystical letters than we Christians, who cast a more careless eye on these common hieroglyphics, and disdain to suck divinity from the flowers of nature. Nor do I so forget God as to adore the name of nature, which I define not with the Schools, the principle of motion and rest, but that straight and regular line, that settled and constant course the wisdom of God hath ordained the actions of his creatures, according to their several kinds. To make a revolution every day is the nature of the sun, because it is that necessary course which God hath ordained it, from which it cannot swerve but by a faculty from that voice which first did give it motion. Now this course of nature God seldom alters or perverts, but like an excellent artist hath so contrived his work that with the selfsame instrument, without a new creation, he may effect his obscurest designs. Thus he sweetened the water with a wood,[2] preserved the creatures in the ark, which the blast of his mouth might have as easily created; for God is like a skilful geometrician, who, when more easily and with one stroke of his compass he might describe or divide a right line, had yet rather do this[3] in a circle or longer way, according to the constituted and forelaid principles of his art; yet this rule of his he doth sometimes pervert, to acquaint the world with his prerogative, lest the arrogancy of our reason should question his power, and conclude he could not; and thus I call the effects of nature the works of God, whose hand and instrument she only is; and therefore to ascribe his actions unto her is to devolve the honour of the principal agent upon the instrument; which if with reason we may do, then let our hammers rise up and boast they have built our houses, and our pens receive the honour of our writings. I hold there is a general beauty in the works of God, and therefore no deformity in any kind or species of creature whatsoever. I cannot tell by what logic we call a toad, a bear, or an elephant ugly, they being created in those outward shapes and figures which best express the actions of their inward forms, and having passed that general visitation of God, who saw that all that he had made was good, that is, conformable to his will, which abhors deformity, and is the rule

---

1] standing still (Joshua 10:12-13)   2] (Exodus 15:25)   3] work through human agency (Noah, Moses)

of order and beauty. There is no deformity but in monstrosity, wherein notwithstanding there is a kind of beauty, nature so ingeniously contriving those irregular parts as they become sometimes more remarkable than the principal fabric. To speak yet more narrowly, there was never anything ugly or misshapen but the Chaos;[4] wherein notwithstanding, to speak strictly, there was no deformity, because no form; nor was it yet impregnate by the voice of God. Now nature is not at variance with art, nor art with nature; they being both the servants of his providence. Art is the perfection of nature. Were the world now as it was the sixth day, there were yet a Chaos. Nature hath made one world, and art another. In brief, all things are artificial, for nature is the art of God.

RM I.16

¶ Philosophical distractions

I confess I have perused them all, and can discover nothing that may startle a discreet belief; yet are there heads carried off with the wind and breath of such motives. I remember a doctor in physic of Italy who could not perfectly believe the immortality of the soul because Galen seemed to make a doubt thereof. With another I was familiarly acquainted in France, a divine and man of singular parts that on the same point was so plunged and gravelled with three lines of Seneca,[1] that all our antidotes, drawn from both and philosophy, could not expel the poison of his error. There are a set of heads that can credit the relations of mariners, yet question the testimony of St Paul; and peremptorily maintain the traditions of Aelian or Pliny, yet in histories of Scripture raise queries and objections, believing no more than they can parallel in human authors. I confess there are in Scripture stories that do exceed the fables of poets, and to a captious reader sound like *Gargantua*[2] or *Bevis*.[3] Search all the legends of times past, and the fabulous conceits of these present, and 'twill be hard to find one that deserves to carry the buckler unto Sampson;[4] yet is all this of an easy

4] primordial matter from which the earth was made

1] 'After death is nothing, and death is itself nothing. Death indivisible is harmful to the body, but not to the suffering of the spirit. We die wholly and no part of us remains.' (*Troad* 399)   2] *Gargantua and Pantagruel* (1532-52), François Rabelais' bawdy mock-epic mock romance   3] *Bevis of Hampton*, a medieval romance   4] i.e. to resemble Sampson

possibility if we conceive a divine concourse or an influence but from the little finger of the Almighty. It is impossible that, either in the discourse of man, or in the infallible voice of God, to the weakness of our apprehension there should not appear irregularities, contradictions, and antinomies. Myself could show a catalogue of doubts never yet imagined nor questioned, as I know, which are not resolved at the first hearing; not queries fantastic, or objections of air; for I cannot hear of atoms in divinity.[5] I can read the story of the pigeon that was sent out of the ark and returned no more, yet not question how she found out her mate that was left behind; that Lazarus was raised from the dead, yet not demand where in the interim his soul awaited; or raise a law case whether his heir might lawfully detain his inheritance bequeathed unto him by his death, and he, though restored to life, have no plea or title unto his former possessions. Whether Eve was framed out of the left side of Adam, I dispute not, because I stand not yet assured which is the right side of a man, or whether there be any such distinction in nature; that she was edified out of the rib of Adam I believe, yet raise no question who shall arise with that rib at the resurrection; whether Adam was an hermaphrodite[6] as the rabbins contend upon the letter of the text, because it is contrary to reason there should be an hermaphrodite before there was a woman, or a composition of two natures, before there was a second composed. Likewise, whether the world was created in autumn, summer, or spring, because it was created in them all; for whatsoever sign the sun possesseth,[7] those four seasons are actually existant; it is the nature of this luminary to distinguish the several seasons of the year, all which it makes at one time in the whole earth, and successively in any part thereof. There are a bundle of curiosities, not only in philosophy, but in divinity, proposed and discussed by men of most supposed abilities, which indeed are not worthy our vacant hours, much less our serious studies; pieces only fit to be placed in Pantagruel's library,[8] or bound up with Tartaretus' *De modo cacandi.*[9]

RM I.21

5] which were a Greek, but not a Biblical, idea   6] 'Male and female created he them' (Genesis 1:27)   7] the sign of the zodiac in which the sun first appeared   8] which contained a great number of preposterous titles (*Gargantua and Pantagruel*, II.7)   9] an imagined treatise by Pierre Tartaret, a fifteenth-century logician, called *Of the Ways of Shitting*

¶ 'The great and true *Amphibium*'

These[1] are certainly the magisterial and masterpieces of the Creator, the flower (or as we may say) the best part of nothing, actually existing[2] what we are but in hopes and probability. We are only[3] that amphibious piece between a corporal and spiritual essence, that middle frame that links those two together and makes good the method of God and nature, that jumps not from extremes but unites the incompatible distances by some middle and participating natures. That we are the breath and similitude of God, it is indisputable and upon record of holy Scripture; but to call ourselves a microcosm or little world, I thought it only a pleasant trope of rhetoric till my nearer judgement and second thoughts told me there was a real truth therein: for first we are a rude mass, and in the rank of creatures which only are, and have a dull kind of being, not yet privileged with life, or preferred[4] to sense or reason; next we live the life of plants, the life of animals, the life of men, and at last the life of spirits, running on in one mysterious nature those five kinds of existences which comprehend the creatures not of the world only, but of the universe; thus is man that great and true amphibium, whose nature is disposed to live not only like other creatures in divers elements, but in divided and distinguished worlds; for though there be but one to sense, there are two to reason; the one visible, the other invisible, whereof Moses seems to have left [no] description; and of the other so obscurely that some parts thereof are yet in controversy;[5] and truly, for those first chapters of Genesis, I must confess a great deal of obscurity, though divines have to the power of human reason endeavoured to make all go in a literal meaning; yet those allegorical interpretations are also probable, and perhaps the mystical method of Moses bred up in the hieroglyphical schools of the Egyptians.[6]

RM I.34

¶ All flesh is grass

Now for the walls of flesh, wherein the soul doth seem to be immured before the resurrection, it is nothing but an elemental composition, and a fabric that must fall to ashes. 'All flesh is grass' is not only meta-

1] angels   2] being in reality   3] alone   4] elevated   5] i.e. fire, which is not referred in the account of the creation of the world in Genesis 6] i.e. Hermetical philosophy (Acts 7:22)

phorically, but literally true, for all those creatures we behold are but the herbs of the field, digested into flesh in them, or more remotely carnified in ourselves. Nay, further, we are what we all abhor, anthropophagi[1] and cannibals, devourers not only of men, but of ourselves; and that not in an allegory, but a positive truth; for all this mass of flesh which we behold came in at our mouths; this frame we look upon hath been upon our trenchers. In brief, we have devoured ourselves. I cannot believe the wisdom of Pythagoras did ever positively and in a literal sense affirm his metempsychosis,[2] or impossible transmigration of the souls of men into beasts; of all metamorphoses and transformations, I believe only one, that is of Lot's wife, for that of Nebuchadnezzar proceeded not so far. In all others I conceive there is no further verity than is contained in their implicit sense and morality: I believe that the whole frame of a beast doth perish and is left in the same state after death, as before it was materialed[3] unto life; that the souls of men know neither contrary nor corruption, that they subsist beyond the body, and outlive death by the privilege of their proper natures, and without a miracle; that the souls of the faithful as they leave earth take possession of heaven; that those apparitions and ghosts of departed persons are not the wandering souls of men but the unquiet walks of devils, prompting and suggesting us unto mischief, blood, and villainy, instilling and stealing into our hearts that the blessed spirits are not at rest in their graves, but wander solicitous of the affairs of the world. That those phantasms appear often and do frequent cemeteries, charnel houses, and churches, it is because those are the dormitories of the dead, where the devil like an insolent champion beholds with pride the spoils and trophies of his victory in Adam.

RM I.37

¶ Chaos and the womb

Some divines count Adam thirty years old at his creation, because they suppose him created in the perfect age and stature of man; and surely we are all out of the computation of our age, and every man is some months elder than he bethinks him; for we live, move, have a being, and are subject to the actions of the elements and the malice of diseases in that other world, the truest microcosm, the womb of our mother. For besides that general and common existence we are

1] man-caters   2] transmigration of the soul into a new body at death
3]* brought into material form

conceived to hold in our chaos, and whilst we sleep within the bosom of our causes,[1] we enjoy a being and life in three distinct worlds wherein we receive most manifest graduations: in that obscure world and womb of our mother our time is short, computed by the moon, yet longer than the days of many creatures that behold the sun; ourselves being yet not without life, sense, and reason; though for the manifestation of its[2] actions it awaits the opportunity of objects, and seems to live there but in its root and soul of vegetation. Entering afterwards upon the scene of the world, we arise up and become another creature, performing the reasonable actions of man, and obscurely manifesting that part of divinity in us, but not in complement and perfection, till we have once more cast our secundine,[3] that is, this slough of flesh, and are delivered into the last world, the ineffable place of Paul,[4] that proper *ubi*[5] of spirits. The smattering I have of the Philosopher's Stone,[6] (which is something more than the perfect exaltation of gold) hath taught me a great deal of divinity, and instructed my belief how that immortal spirit and incorruptible substance of my soul may lie obscure, and sleep awhile within this house of flesh. Those strange and mystical transmigrations that I have observed in silkworms turned my philosophy into divinity. There is in those works of nature which seem to puzzle reason, something divine, and hath more in it than the eye of a common spectator doth discover.

RM I.39

¶ Of death

.... surely there is no torture to the rack of a disease, nor any poiniards in death itself like those in the way and prologue unto it. *Emori nolo, sed me esse mortuum nihil curo,*[1] I would not die, but care not to be dead. Were I of Caesar's religion I should be of his desires, and wish rather to go off at one blow than to be sawed in pieces by the grating torture of a disease. Men that look no further than their outsides think health an appurtenance unto life, and quarrel with their constitutions for being sick; but I that have examined the parts of man and know

---

1] before we have form   2] reason's   3] afterbirth   4] paradise (II Corinthians 12:3-4)   5] place (from L. 'where')   6] the substance believed by alchemists to have the power of changing all other substances into silver or gold; used here, perhaps, to mean 'mystical philosophy'

1] Cicero, *Tusculan Disputations*

upon what tender filaments that fabric hangs, do wonder that we are not always so, and considering the thousand doors that lead to death do thank my God that we can die but once. 'Tis not only the mischief of diseases and the villainy of poisons that make an end of us; we vainly accuse the fury of guns, and the new inventions of death. 'Tis in the power of every hand to destroy us, and we are beholding unto every-one we meet he doth not kill us. There is therefore but one comfort left, that though it be in the power of the weakest arm to take away life, it is not in the strongest to deprive us of death. God would not exempt himself from that: the misery of immortality in the flesh he undertook not, that was in it immortal. Certainly there is no happiness within this circle of flesh, nor is it in the optics of these eyes to behold felicity. The first day of our jubilee[2] is death; the devil hath therefore failed of his desires; we are happier with death than we should have been without it. There is no misery but in himself where there is no end of misery; and so indeed in his own sense the Stoic is in the right: he forgets that he can die who complains of misery; we are in the power of no calamity while death is in our own.

RM I.44

¶ Last things

I believe the world draws near its end,[1] yet is neither old nor decayed, nor will ever perish upon the ruins of its own principles.[2] As the creation was a work above nature, so is its adversary, annihilation, without which the world hath not its end, but its mutation. Now, what fire should be able to consume it thus far without the breath of God, which is the truest consuming flame, my philosophy cannot inform me. Some believe there went not a minute to the world's creation, nor shall there go to its destruction; those six days so punctually described, make not to them one moment, but rather seem to manifest the method and idea of that great work in the intellect of God, than the manner how he proceeded in its operation. I cannot dream that there should be at the last day any such judicial proceeding, or calling to the bar, as indeed the Scripture seems to imply, and the literal commentators do conceive; for unspeakable mysteries in the Scriptures are often delivered in a vulgar and illustrative way, and being written unto man,

2] year of emancipation or restoration

1] the apocalypse   2] constituent parts; i.e. God will destroy it

are delivered not as they truly are but as they may be understood;
wherein, notwithstanding the different interpretations according to
different capacities, may stand firm with our devotion, nor be any way
prejudicial to each single edification.[3]

RM I.45

¶ Resurrection of the whole body

How the dead shall arise is no question of my faith; to believe only
possibilities is not faith, but mere philosophy; many things are true in
divinity which are neither inducible by reason nor confirmable by
sense; and many things in philosophy confirmable by sense yet not
inducible by reason. Thus it is impossible by any solid or demonstra-
tive reasons to persuade a man to believe the conversion of the needle[1]
to the north, though this be possible and true and easily credible, upon
a single experiment unto the sense. I believe that our estranged and
divided ashes shall unite again; that our separated dust after so many
pilgrimages and transformations into the parts of minerals, plants,
animals, elements, shall at the voice of God return unto their primitive
shapes, and join again to make up their primary and predestinated[2]
forms.[3] As at the creation there was a separation of that confused mass
into its species, so at the destruction thereof there shall be a separation
into its distinct individuals. As at the creation of the world all the
distinct species that we behold lay involved in one mass till the fruitful
voice of God separated this united multitude into its several species, so
at the last day, when these corrupted relics shall be scattered in the
wilderness of forms and seem to have forgot their proper habits, God
by a powerful voice shall command them back into their proper shapes
and call them out by their single individuals. Then shall appear the
fertility of Adam, and the magic of that sperm that hath dilated into so
many millions. I have often beheld as a miracle that artificial resurrection and revivification of mercury, how being mortified[4] into thousand shapes, it assumes again its own, and returns to its numerical self.[5]
Let us speak naturally and like philosophers: the forms of alterable

3] all interpretations of Scripture are valid because all are 'tropical'

1] compass needle   2] before death, before judgement was made upon them
3] in Scholastic philosophy, the essential determining principle of a thing; these
exist separately from things, and need not be embodied   4] dissolved in acid
5] unified whole

bodies in these sensible corruptions[6] perish not; nor, as we imagine, wholly quit their mansions, but retire and contract themselves into their secret and inaccessible parts, where they may best protect themselves from the action of their antagonist. A plant or vegetable consumed to ashes, to a contemplative and School philosopher,[7] seems utterly destroyed, and the form to have taken his leave forever; but to a sensible artist[8] the forms are not perished, but withdrawn into their incombustible part, where they lie secure from the action of that devouring element. This is made good by experience, which can from the ashes of a plant revive the plant, and from its cinders recall it into its stalk and leaves again. What the art of man can do in these inferior pieces, what blasphemy is it to affirm the finger of God cannot do in these more perfect and sensible structures?[9] This is that mystical philosophy,[10] from whence no true scholar becomes an atheist, but from the visible effects of nature grows up a real divine, and beholds not in a dream, as Ezekiel,[11] but in an ocular and visible object the types of his resurrection.

RM I.48

¶ Election

Again, I am confident and fully persuaded, yet dare not take my oath, of my salvation; I am as it were sure, and do believe without all doubt, that there is such a city as Constantinople; yet for me to take my oath thereon were a kind of perjury because I hold no infallible warrant from my own sense to confirm me in the certainty thereof. And truly, though many pretend an absolute certainty of their salvation, yet when an humble soul shall contemplate her own unworthiness she shall meet with many doubts and suddenly find how much we stand in need of the precept of St Paul, 'Work out your salvation with fear and trembling.' That which is the cause of my election[1] I hold to be the

6] physical decay (as opposed to the incorruptibility of form, which withdraws but cannot perish)   7] whose authorities were the Church Fathers and Aristotle, and whose primary subjects were logic, metaphysics, and divinity   8] an experimentalist   9] mankind   10] the Hermetic philosophy of signatures and of types, which finds intimations of God's cosmic design in the minor examples of nature   11] in Ezekiel's prophetic dream of resurrection, in which scattered bones are reunited and fleshed out (Ezekiel 37:1)

1] predestined by God to be saved

cause of my salvation, which was the mercy and beneplacit[2] of God before I was, or the foundation of the world. 'Before Abraham was, I am,' is the saying of Christ; yet is it true in some sense if I say it of myself, for I was not only before myself, but Adam, that is, in the idea of God,[3] and the decree of that synod[4] held from all eternity. And in this sense, I say, the world was before the creation, and at an end before it had a beginning; and thus was I dead before I was alive. Though my grave be England, my dying place was Paradise, and Eve miscarried of me before she conceived of Cain.

RM I.59

¶A community in learning

But to return from philosophy to charity, I hold not so narrow a conceit of this virtue as to conceive that to give alms is only to be charitable, or think a piece of liberality can comprehend the total of charity;[1] divinity hath wisely divided the acts thereof into many branches and hath taught us in this narrow way[2] many paths unto goodness. As many ways as we may do good, so many ways we may be charitable. There are infirmities, not only of body, but of soul and fortunes, which do require the merciful hand of our abilities. I cannot contemn a man for his ignorance but behold him with as much pity as I do Lazarus.[3] It is no greater charity to clothe his body than apparel the nakedness of his soul. It is an honourable object to see the reasons of other men wear our liveries, and their borrowed understandings do homage to the bounty of ours. It is the cheapest way of beneficence, and like the natural charity of the sun illuminates another without obscuring itself. To be reserved and caitiff[4] in this part of goodness is the sordidest piece of covetousness, and more contemptible than pecuniary avarice. To this (as calling myself a scholar) I am obliged by the duty of my condition. I make not therefore my head a grave, but a treasure of knowledge; I intend no monopoly, but a community in learning; I

2] gracious purpose   3] the image and form of a thing as it exists in the mind of God   4] the unified voice of the Trinity, which Browne imagines as a kind of council, which decreed the creation of man (Genesis 1:26)

1] simple munificence does not adequately fulfill the meaning of the term charity in (I Corinthians 13), which is love of fellow man   2] the simple giving of alms as an expression of Christian charity   3] a beggar full of sores who was comforted in heaven (Luke 16:20-23)   4] mean

study not for my own sake only, but for theirs that study not for themselves. I envy no man that knows more than myself, but pity those that know less. I instruct no man as an exercise of my knowledge, or with intent rather to nourish and keep it alive in mine own head than beget and propagate it in his; and in the midst of all my endeavours there is but one thought that dejects me, that my acquired parts[5] must perish with myself nor can be legacied among my honoured friends. I cannot fall out or contemn a man for an error or conceive why a difference in opinion should divide our affection; for controversies, disputes, and argumentations, both in philosophy and in divinity, if they meet with discreet and peaceable natures, do not infringe the laws of charity; in all disputes, so much as there is of passion, so much there is of nothing to the purpose; for then reason like a bad hound spends[6] upon a false scent and forsakes the question first started. And this is one reason why controversies are never determined, for though they be amply proposed, they are scarce at all handled;[7] they do so swell with unnecessary digressions, and the parentheses on the party[8] is often as large as the main discourse upon the subject. The foundations of religion are already established, and the principles of salvation subscribed unto by all; there remain not many controversies worth a passion, and yet never any disputed without, not only in divinity, but in inferior arts: What a βατραχομυομαχία[9] and hot skirmish is betwixt S. and T.[10] in Lucian? How do grammarians hack and slash for the genitive case in Jupiter?[11] How do they break their own pates to save that of Priscian?[12] *Si foret in terris, rideret Democritus.*[13] Yea, even amongst wiser militants how many wounds have been given and credits stained for the poor victory of an opinion or beggarly conquest of a distinction? Scholars are men of peace – they bear no arms – but their tongues are sharper than Actius his razor;[14] their pens carry farther and give a louder report than thunder; I had rather stand the shock of a basilisco,[15] than the fury of a merciless pen.

5] learning and understanding   6] barks   7] although there is much discussion, no use is made of it   8] part (of the subject)   9] batrachomyomachia, the battle between frogs and mice described in an ancient mock-heroic poem   10] a courtroom debate between the consonants sigma and tau in *The Consonants at Law* by Lucian   11] 'Whether *Jovis* or *Jupiteris.*'   12] 'breaking Priscian's head' means to violate the rules of grammar   13] 'If he were on earth, Democritus would laugh'   14] a soothsayer who encouraged Tarquin, a king of Rome, to cleave a whetstone with a razor   15] a large brass cannon

It is not mere zeal to learning, or devotion to the Muses, that wiser princes patron the arts and carry an indulgent aspect unto scholars, but a desire to have their names eternised by the memory of their writings, and a fear of the revengeful pen of succeeding ages: for these are the men that when they have played their parts and had their exits must step out and give the moral of their scenes,[16] and deliver unto posterity an inventory of their virtues and vices. And surely there goes a great deal of conscience to the compiling of an history; there is no reproach to the scandal of a story: it is such an authentic kind of falsehood that with authority belies our good names to all nations and posterity.

RM II.3

¶ Of harmony

I was never yet once married,[1] and commend their resolutions who never marry twice. Not that I disallow of second marriage, as neither in[2] all cases of polygamy, which considering sometimes and the unequal number of both sexes may be also necessary. The whole woman was made for man, but the twelfth part of man[3] for woman. Man is the whole world and the breath of God, woman the rib and crooked piece of man. I could be content that we might procreate like trees, without conjunction, or that there were any way to perpetuate the world without this trivial and vulgar way of coition. It is the foolishest act a wise man commits in all his life, nor is there anything that will more deject his cooled imagination when he shall consider what an odd and unworthy piece of folly he hath committed. I speak not in prejudice, nor am [I] averse from that sweet sex, but naturally amorous of all that is beautiful. I can look a whole day with delight upon a handsome picture, though it be but of an horse.

It is my temper, and I like it better, to affect all harmony; and sure there is music even in beauty, and the silent note which Cupid strikes, far sweeter than the sound of an instrument. For there is a music wherever there is a harmony, order, or proportion; and thus far we may maintain the music of the spheres,[4] for those well-ordered

16] like choric presenters of plays, the scholars must offer summaries of and judgements on the lives of their patrons

1] *Religio Medici* was written in the mid-1630s; Browne married in 1641.
2] neither do I disallow   3] alluding to the number of ribs in humans
4] in Ptolemaic astronomy, the heavenly concentric crystalline spheres revolved and produced divine harmonies

motions and regular paces, though they give no sound unto the ear, yet to the understanding they strike a note most full of harmony. Whosoever is harmonically composed delights in harmony, which makes me much distrust the symmetry of those heads which declaim against all church music.[5] For myself, not only from my obedience but my particular genius, I do embrace it; for even that vulgar and tavern music, which makes one man merry, another mad, strikes me into a deep fit of devotion and a profound contemplation of the first composer; there is something in it of divinity more than the ear discovers. It is an hieroglyphical and shadowed lesson of the whole world[6] and the creatures of God; such a melody to the ear, as the whole world well understood, would afford[7] the understanding. In brief, it is a sensible fit[8] of that harmony which intellectually sounds in the ears of God. I will not say, with Plato, the soul is an harmony, but harmonical,[9] and hath its nearest sympathy[10] unto music. Thus some, whose temper of body agrees and humours the constitution of their souls, are born poets, though indeed all are naturally inclined unto rhythm. This made Tacitus in the very first line of his story fall upon verse; and Cicero, the worst of poets, but declaiming for a poet,[11] falls in the very first sentence upon a perfect hexameter.

I feel not in me those sordid and unchristian desires of my profession: I do not secretly implore and wish for plagues, rejoice at famines, revolve ephemerides,[12] and almanacs in expectation of malignant aspects, fatal conjunctions, and eclipses, I rejoice not at unwholesome springs, nor unseasonable winters; my prayers go with the husbandman's; I desire everything in its proper season, that neither men nor the times be out of temper. Let me be sick myself if oftentimes that malady of my patient be not a disease unto me. I desire rather to cure his infirmities than my own necessities. Where I do him no good methinks it is scarce honest gain, though I confess 'tis but the worthy salary[13] of our well-intended endeavours. I am not only ashamed but heartily sorry that besides death there are diseases incurable; yet not for my own sake, or that they be beyond my art, but for the general cause and sake of humanity, whose common cause I apprehend as mine own. And to speak more generally, those three noble professions which all civil commonwealths do honour are raised upon

5] which was thought by some sects to be an affectation   6] the order expressed by music is symbolic of the order inherent in the creation   7] further
8] a section of a piece of music   9] not harmonious but nevertheless sympathetic to all that *is*   10] occult correspondence between things
11] in *Pro Archia Poeta*   12] astronomical tables   13] the doctor's fee

the fall of Adam, and are not any exempt from their infirmities. There are not only diseases incurable in physic, but cases indissoluble in law, vices incorrigible in divinity: if general councils[14] may err, I do not see why particular courts should be infallible –their perfectest rules are raised upon the erroneous reason of man, and the laws of one do but condemn the rules of another; as Aristotle oftimes the opinions of his predecessors because, though agreeable to reason, yet were not consonant to his own rules and the logic of his proper principles. Again, to speak nothing of the sin against the Holy Ghost,[15] whose cure not only but whose nature is unknown, I can cure the gout and stone in some sooner than divinity, pride, or avarice in others. I can cure vices by physic, when they remain incurable by divinity, and shall obey my pills when they contemn their precepts.[16] I boast nothing, but plainly say we all labour against our own cure, for death is the cure of all diseases. There is no catholicon or universal remedy I know but this, which though nauseous to queasier stomachs, yet to prepared appetites is nectar and a pleasant potion of immortality.

RM II.9

¶Man and microcosm

Now for my life, it is a miracle of thirty years, which to relate were not a history but a piece of poetry, and would sound to common ears like a fable. For the world, I count it not an inn but an hospital, and a place not to live but to die in. The world that I regard is myself: it is the microcosm of mine own frame that I cast mine eye on; for the other,[1] I use it but like my globe, and turn it round sometimes for my recreation. Men that look upon my outside, perusing only my condition and fortunes, do err in my altitude,[2] for I am above Atlas[3] his shoulders. The earth is a point not only in respect of the heavens above us, but of that heavenly and celestial part within us. That mass of flesh that circumscribes me limits not my mind; that surface[4] that tells the heavens it hath an end cannot persuade me I have any. I take my circle to be

14] 'General councils...may err..., even in things pertaining unto God.' (Articles of Religion, 21)   15] blasphemy, which cannot be forgiven (Matthew 12:31-2)   16] when physic seems to contradict the precepts of divines

1] the earth   2] judge me incorrectly   3] a Titan who supported the world on his shoulders   4] the crystalline sphere within which the earth is fixed and immobile, in Ptolemaic cosmology

above three hundred and sixty;[5] though the number of the arc[6] do measure my body, it comprehendeth not my mind. Whilst I study to find how I am a microcosm or little world, I find myself something more than the great. There is surely a piece of divinity in us, something that was before the elements and owes no homage unto the sun. Nature tells me I am the image of God as well as Scripture; he that understands not thus much, hath not his introduction or first lesson and is yet to begin the alphabet of man. Let me not injure the felicity of others if I say I am as happy as any. *Ruat coelum, fiat voluntas tua*[7] salveth all, so that whatsoever happens, it is but what our daily prayers desire.

RM II.11

¶ Alms and avarice

... to me avarice seems not so much a vice as a deplorable piece of madness; to conceive ourselves urinals,[1] or be persuaded that we are dead, is not so ridiculous nor so many degrees beyond the power of hellebore[2] as this. The opinions of theory and positions of men are not so void of reason as their practised conclusions. Some have held that snow is black, that the earth moves, that the soul is air, fire, water;[3] but all this is philosophy, and there is no delirium[4] if we do but speculate[5] the folly and indisputable dotage of avarice. To that subterraneous idol and god of the earth,[6] I do confess I am an atheist. I cannot persuade myself to honour that [which] the world adores. Whatsoever virtue its prepared substance may have within my body,[7] it hath no influence nor operation without. I would not entertain a base design or an action that should call me villain for the Indies, and for this only do I love and honour my own soul and have, methinks, two arms too few to embrace myself. Aristotle is too severe that will not allow us to be truly liberal without wealth and the bountiful hand of fortune; if

5] i.e. I am infinite   6] the number of degrees in a circle   7] 'Let the sky fall; your will be done'

1] To think one's self a urinal (a clear glass vessel used by physicians in uroscopy – diagnosis by examination of urine) was both metaphorically and delusionally a sign of melancholy   2] medicine believed to cure insanity, of which avarice is an extreme form   3] suspect positions advanced by Anaxagoras and Diogenes, Democritus, and Hippon   4] absurd ideas, especially avaricious ones
5] consider   6] gold, or, figuratively, the god of gold (Mammon)
7] gold was administered medicinally

this be true, I must confess I am charitable only in my liberal intentions and bountiful well-wishes. But if the example of the mite[8] be not only an act of wonder but an example of the noblest charity, surely poor men may also build hospitals, and the rich alone have not erected cathedrals. I have a private method which others observe not: I take the opportunity of myself to do good; I borrow the occasion of charity from mine own necessities, and supply the wants of others when I am most in need myself; for it is an honest stratagem to take advantage of ourselves and so to husband the acts of virtue, that where they are defective in one circumstance, they may repay their want and multiply their goodness in another. I have not Peru[9] in my desires, but a competence and ability to perform those good works to which the Almighty hath inclined my nature. He is rich who hath enough to be charitable, and it is hard to be so poor that a noble mind may not find a way to this piece of goodness. 'He that gives to the poor lendeth to the Lord'.[10] There is more rhetorick in this one sentence than in a library of sermons, and indeed if these sentences were understood by the reader with the same emphasis as they are delivered by the author, we needed not those volumes of instructions, but might be honest by an epitome.[11]

RM II.13

¶ Precepts for dying

Not to fear death, nor desire it, was short of his[1] resolution; to be dissolved, and be with Christ, was his dying ditty. He conceived his thread long in no long course of years, and when he had scarce outlived the second life of Lazarus,[2] esteeming it enough to approach the years of his Saviour,[3] who so ordered his own human state as not to be old upon earth.

But to be content with death may be better than to desire it: a miserable life may make us wish for death, but a virtuous one to rest in it, which is the advantage of those resolved Christians who, looking on

---

8] from Mark 12:43: doing as much as possible with the least amount   9] source of gold   10] Proverbs 19:17
11] a summary of chief points

1] of Robert Loveday, whose death of consumption at the age of thirty-five is the subject of 'A Letter to a Friend'   2] 'Who upon some accounts...is said to have lived thirty years after he was raised by our Saviour.'   3] by tradition, thirty-three

death not only as the sting, but the period and end of sin, the horizon and isthmus between this life and a better, and the death of this world but as a nativity of another, do contentedly submit unto the common necessity, and envy not Enoch or Elias.[4]

Not to be content with life is the unsatisfactory state of those which destroy themselves, who, being afraid to live, run blindly upon their own death, which no man fears by experience; and the Stoics had a notable doctrine to take away the fear thereof, that is, in such extremities to desire that which is not to be avoided, and wish what might be feared, and so made evils voluntary and to suit with their own desires, which took off the terror of them....

His willingness to leave this world about that age when most men think they may best enjoy it, though paradoxical unto worldly ears, was not strange unto mine who have so often observed that many, though old, oft stick fast unto the world and seem to be drawn, like Cacus's oxen,[5] backward with great struggling and reluctancy unto the grave. The long habit of living makes mere men more hardly to part with life, and all to be nothing but what is to come. To live at the rate of the old world,[6] when some could scarce remember themselves young, may afford no better digested death than a more moderate period. Many would have thought it an happiness to have had their lot of life in some notable conjunctures[7] of ages past; but the uncertainty of future times hath tempted few to make a part in ages to come. And surely, he that hath taken the true altitude of things and rightly calculated the degenerate state of this age is not like to envy those that shall live in the next, much less three or four hundred years hence, when no man can comfortably imagine what face this world will carry; and therefore since every age makes a step unto the end of all things, and the Scripture affords so hard a character of the last times,[8] quiet minds will be content with their generations and rather bless ages past than be ambitious of those to come.

LF 111-12

4] Enoch walked with God and was translated into heaven; Elias (Elijah) ascended into heaven in a fiery chariot enveloped in a whirlwind   5] Cacus, a son of Vulcan, stole from Hercules the magic cattle of Geryon by dragging them backwards into his cave   6] the pre-Noachic period in Genesis, when the antediluvian giant race commonly lived to extraordinary ages   7] crises
8] the Book of Revelation, which describes signs by which the last age before the Apocalypse will be recognized

II. ERROR

¶ Browne to the reader of *Vulgar Errors*

Would truth dispense, we could be content, with Plato, that knowledge were but remembrance; that intellectual acquisition were but reminiscential evocation,[1] and new impressions but the colourishing of old stamps which stood pale in the soul before. For what is worse, knowledge is made by oblivion, and to purchase a clear and warrantable body of truth we must forget and part with much we know, our tender enquiries taking up learning at large, and together with true and assured notions, receiving many wherein our reviewing judgements do find no satisfaction. And therefore in this encyclopaedia and round of knowledge, like the great and exemplary wheels of heaven, we must observe two circles: that while we are daily carried about and whirled on by the swing and rapt of the one, we may maintain a natural and proper course in the slow and sober wheel of the other.[2] And this we shall more readily perform if we timely survey our knowledge, impartially singling out those encroachments which junior compliance and popular credulity hath admitted. Whereof at present we have endeavoured a long and serious adviso,[3] proposing not only a large and copious list, but from experience and reason attempting[4] their decisions....

Nor have we let fall our pen upon discouragement of contradiction, unbelief, and difficulty of dissuasion from radicated[5] beliefs and points of high prescription,[6] although we are very sensible how hardly teaching years do learn, what roots old age contracteth unto errors, and how such as are but acorns in our younger brows grow oaks in our elder heads and become inflexible unto the powerfulest arms of

1] restating of remembered information; Plato advances this model of knowledge in *Phaedo* and *Meno*.   2] the axial and the orbital rotation of celestial bodies; fig., daily experience and received precepts   3] information or piece of intelligence, possibly with the sense of 'counsel' or 'suggestion'   4] questioning   5] established   6] handed down by ancient writers

reason; although we have also beheld what cold requitals others have
found in their several redemptions of truth, and how their ingenuous
enquiries have been dismissed with censure, and obloquy of
singularities[7]....

Our first intentions, considering the common interest of truth,
resolved to propose it unto the Latin republic[8] and equal judges of
Europe; but owing in the first place this service unto our country, and
therein especially unto its ingenuous gentry,[9] we have declared ourself
in a language best conceived,[10] although I confess the quality of the
subject will sometimes carry us into expressions beyond mere English
apprehensions. And indeed, if elegancy still proceedeth, and English
pens maintain that stream we have of late observed to flow from many,
we shall within a few years be fain[11] to learn Latin to understand English, and a work will prove of equal facility in either. Nor have we
addressed our pen or style unto the people (whom books do not re
dress, and are this way incapable of reduction), but unto the knowing
and leading part of learning....

We hope it will not be unconsidered that we find no open tract or
constant manuduction[12] in this labyrinth, but are ofttimes fain to wander in the America and untravelled parts of truth. For though not
many years past Dr Primerose hath made a learned discourse of vulgar
errors in physic, yet have we discussed but two or three thereof. Scipio
Mercurii hath also left an excellent tract in Italian, concerning popular
errors; but confining himself only unto those in physic, he hath little
conduced unto the generality of our doctrine. Laurentius Joubertus
by the same title[13] led our expectation into thoughts of great relief,
whereby notwithstanding we reaped no advantage, it answering scarce
at all the promise of the inscription. Nor perhaps (if it were yet extant)
should we find any farther assistance from that ancient piece of
Andreas pretending the same title.[14] And therefore we are often constrained to stand alone against the strength of opinion, and to meet
the Goliah and giant of authority with contemptible pibbles[15] and
feeble arguments, drawn from the scrip[16] and slender stock of ourselves. Nor have we indeed scarce named any author whose name we

7] the disgrace of going against accepted beliefs   8] European men of letters
who communicate in Latin rather than vernacular languages   9] the literate
landowning class (i.e. not the scholarly cadre)   10] understood   11] obliged
12] path or assistance   13] respectively, these works are *Vulgar Errors in Medicine* (1639); *Popular Errors of Italy* (1603); and *De Vulgi Erroribus* (1600)
14] apparently, a book of superstitious beliefs   15] pebbles   16] a small
wallet or satchel, especially carried by a pilgrim or beggar

do not honour; and if detraction could invite us, discretion surely would contain us from any derogatory intention where highest pens and friendliest eloquence must fail in commendation.[17]

And therefore also we cannot but hope the equitable considerations and candour of reasonable minds. We cannot expect the frown of theology herein; nor can they which behold the present state of things and controversy of points so long received in divinity condemn our sober enquiries in the doubtful appurtenances of arts[18] and receptaries[19] of philosophy. Surely philologers and critical discoursers, who look beyond the shell and obvious exteriors of things, will not be angry with our narrower explorations. And we cannot doubt our brothers in physic (whose knowledge in naturals[20] will lead them into a nearer apprehension of many things delivered) will friendly accept, if not countenance, our endeavours. Nor can we conceive it may be unwelcome unto those honoured worthies who endeavour the advancement of learning, as being likely to find a clearer progression, when so many rubs are levelled, and many untruths taken off (which, passing as principles with common beliefs, disturb the tranquillity of axioms) which otherwise might be raised. And wise men cannot but know that arts and learning want this expurgation; and if the course of truth be permitted unto itself, like that of time and uncorrected computations,[21] it cannot escape many errors which duration still enlargeth.

Lastly, we are not magisterial in opinions, nor have we, dictatorlike, obtruded our conceptions; but in the humility of enquiries or disquisitions have only proposed them unto more ocular discerners.[22] And therefore opinions are free, and open it is for any to think or declare the contrary. And we shall so far encourage contradiction as to promise no disturbance or reoppose any pen that shall fallaciously or captiously refute us, that shall only lay hold of our lapses, single out digressions, corollaries, or ornamental conceptions[23] to evidence his own in as indifferent truths; and shall only take notice of such whose experimental and judicious knowledge shall solemnly look upon it, not only to destroy of ours but to establish of his own, not to traduce or extenuate but to explain and dilucidate,[24] to add and ampliate, according to the laudable custom of the ancients in their sober

17] the best praise cannot sufficiently extol the virtues of our authorities
18] questionable conclusions of human knowledge   19] accepted notions
20] natural phenomena   21] the Julian calendar, established by Julius Caesar in
46 BC, had to be corrected in 1582 by Pope Gregory XIII   22] experimentalists
and observers   23] metaphorical descriptions   24] make clear

promotions of learning. Unto whom notwithstanding we shall not contentiously rejoin, or[25] only to justify our own, but to applaud or confirm his maturer assertions, and shall confer what is in us unto his name and honour, ready to be swallowed in any worthy enlarger, as having acquired our end, if any way or under any name we may obtain a work so much desired and yet[26] desiderated of truth.

PE 3-6

¶The disposition of the people to error

....For the assured truth of things is derived from the principles of knowledge and causes, which determine their verities. Whereof their uncultivated understandings, scarce holding any theory, they are but bad discerners of verity; and in the numerous track of error but casually do hit the point and unity of truth.

Their understanding is so feeble in the discernment of falsities and averting the errors of reason, that it submitteth unto the fallacies of sense and is unable to rectify the error of its sensations. Thus the greater part of mankind, having but one eye of sense and reason, conceive the earth far bigger than the sun, the fixed stars lesser than the moon, their figures plain, and their spaces from earth equidistant. For thus their sense informeth them, and herein their reason cannot rectify them; and therefore hopelessly continuing in mistakes, they live and die in their absurdities, passing their days in perverted apprehensions and conceptions of the world derogatory unto God and the wisdom of the creation....

And therefore are they led rather by example than precept, receiving persuasions from visible inducements before intellectual instructions. And therefore also they judge of human actions by the event; for being uncapable of operable circumstances,[1] or rightly to judge the prudentiality of affairs, they only gaze upon the visible success, and thereafter condemn or cry up the whole progression.[2] And so from this ground in the lecture of Holy Scripture their apprehensions are commonly confined unto the literal sense of the text, from whence have ensued the gross and duller sort of heresies. For not attaining the deuteroscopy[3] and second intention of the words, they are fain to omit

25] or do so   26] still

1] unable to consider external factors   2] incapable of evaluating the wisdom of actions, they take into account only their consequences   3]* ulterior meaning their superconsequencies, coherencies, figures, or tropologies,[4] and are not sometime persuaded by fire beyond their literalities. And therefore also things invisible but unto intellectual discernments, to humour the grossness of their comprehensions have been degraded from their proper forms, and God himself dishonoured into manual expressions.[5] And so likewise being unprovided or unsufficient for higher speculations, they will always betake themselves unto sensible representations, and can hardly be restrained the dullness of idolatry. A sin or folly not only derogatory unto God but men, overthrowing their reason as well as his divinity; in brief, a reciprocation or rather an inversion of the creation, making God one way as he made us another – that is, after our image, as he made us after His own....

PE I.iii.26-7

¶Credulity and sedentary curiosity

....And as credulity is the cause of error, so incredulity oftentimes of not enjoying truth; and that not only an obstinate incredulity, whereby we will not acknowledge assent unto what is reasonably inferred, but any academical reservation in matters of easy truth, or rather sceptical infidelity against the evidence of reason and sense. For these are conceptions befalling wise men, as absurd as the apprehensions of fools and the credulity of the people which promiscuously swallow anything. For this is not only derogatory unto the wisdom of God, who hath proposed the world unto our knowledge, and thereby the notion of Himself, but also detractory unto the intellect and sense of man, expressedly disposed for that inquisition, and therefore *hoc tantum scio, quod nihil scio*[1] is not to be received in an absolute sense, but is comparatively expressed unto the number of things whereof our knowledge is ignorant. Nor will it acquit the insatisfaction of those which quarrel with all things, or dispute matters concerning whose verities we have conviction from reason or decision from the inerrable and requisite conditions of sense. And therefore if any affirm the earth doth move and will not believe with us it standeth still,[2] because he

4] respectively, secondary meanings;** contexts; rhetorical, not literal, expressions; metaphors   5] concrete images and renderings of inexpressible or intellectual truths in divinity

1] 'I know only that I know nothing', a standard phrase usually attributed to Socrates   2] Browne did not accept the Copernican model of heliocentrism

hath probable reasons for it and I no infallible sense nor reason against it, I will not quarrel with his assertion. But if, like Zeno,[3] he shall walk about and yet deny there is any motion in nature, surely that man was constituted for Anticyra[4] and were a fit companion for those who, having a conceit they are dead, cannot be convicted[5] into the society of the living....

The fourth is a supinity or neglect of enquiry, even of matters whereof we doubt; rather believing than going to see; or doubting with ease and *gratis* than believing with difficulty or purchase. Whereby, either from a temperamental inactivity we are unready to put in execution the suggestions or dictates of reason, or by a content and acquiescence in every species of truth, we embrace the shadow thereof, or so much as may palliate its just and substantial acquirements. Had our forefathers sat down in these resolutions, or had their curiosities been sedentary who pursued the knowledge of things through all the corners of nature, the face of truth had been obscure unto us, whose lustre in some part their industries have revealed.

Certainly the sweat of their labours was not salt unto them, and they took delight in the dust of their endeavours. For questionless, in knowledge there is no slender difficulty; and truth, which wise men say doth lie in a well, is not recoverable, but by exantlation.[6] It were some extenuation of the curse[7] if *In sudore vultus tui*[8] were confinable unto corporal exercitations, and there still remained a paradise or unthorny place of knowledge.[9] But now our understandings being eclipsed, as well as our tempers infirmed, we must betake ourselves to ways of reparation and depend upon the illumination of our endeavours. For thus we may in some measure repair our primary ruins[10] and build ourselves men again. And though the attempts of some have been precipitous, and their enquiries so audacious as to come within command of the flaming swords[11] and lost themselves in attempts above humanity, yet have the enquiries of most defected by the way and tired within the sober circumference of knowledge....

PE I.v.37-9

3] whose paradox of the arrow and of Achilles and the tortoise showed that motion is impossible   4] a town in central Greece famous for its hellebore, a plant used to treat insanity   5] overcome and forced   6] drawing out   7] the fall of man   8] 'in the sweat of thy face' (Genesis 3:19)   9] in consequence of the fall of man, all kinds of human labour, including intellectual, was thought to have become difficult   10] our initial failure (i.e. in the fall of man)   11] sent by God to drive Adam and Eve out of Eden and to guard the tree of life (Genesis 3:24)

¶ Of adherence and prostration unto antiquity

But the mortalest enemy unto knowledge, and that which hath done
the greatest execution upon truth, hath been a peremptory adhesion
unto authority, and more especially the establishing of our belief upon
the dictates of antiquity. For (as every capacity may observe) most men
of ages present so superstitiously do look on ages past that the authorities of the one exceed the reasons of the other, whose persons indeed
being far removed from our times, their works, which seldom with us
pass uncontrolled,[1] either by contemporaries or immediate successors,
are now become out of the distance of envies,[2] and the farther removed from present times are conceived to approach the nearer unto
truth itself. Now hereby methinks we manifestly delude ourselves, and
widely walk out of the track of truth.

For first, men hereby impose a thralldom on their times, which the
ingenuity of no age should endure, or indeed, the presumption of any
did ever yet enjoin. Thus Hippocrates about two thousand years ago
conceived it no injustice either to examine or refute the doctrines of
his predecessors; Galen the like; and Aristotle the most of any. Yet did
not any of these conceive themselves infallible, or set down their dictates as verities irrefragable, but when they deliver their own inventions or reject other men's opinions they proceed with judgement and
ingenuity, establishing their assertions not only with great solidity but
submitting them also unto the correction of future discovery.

Secondly, men that adore times past consider not that those times
were once present – that is, as they unto us at present. As we rely on
them, even so will those on us and magnify us hereafter who at present
condemn ourselves, which very absurdity is daily committed amongst
us, even in the esteem and censure of our own times. And to speak
impartially, old men from whom we should expect the greatest example of wisdom do most exceed in this point of folly, commending the
days of their youth which they scarce remember (at least well understood not), extolling those times their younger ears have heard their
fathers condemn, and condemning those times the grey heads of their
posterity shall commend. And thus is it the humour of many heads to
extol the days of their forefathers and declaim against the wickedness
of times present....

Thirdly, the testimonies of antiquity, and such as pass oraculously
amongst us, were not, if we consider them, always so exact as to exam-

1] undisputed   2] reproach

ine the doctrine they delivered. For some, and those the acutest of them, have left unto us many things of falsity, controllable not only by critical and collective reason but common and country[3] observation.

Hereof there want not many examples in Aristotle, through all his book of animals. We shall instance only in three of his problems, and all contained under one section. The first enquireth why a man doth cough, but not an ox or cow; whereas notwithstanding, the contrary is often observed by husbandmen and stands confirmed by those who have expressly treated *de re rustica*,[4] and have also delivered divers remedies for it. Why juments,[5] such as horse, oxen, and asses, have no eructation or belching, whereas indeed the contrary is often observed, and also delivered by Columella. And thirdly, why man alone hath grey hairs, whereas it cannot escape the eyes and ordinary observation of all men as horses, dogs, and foxes wax grey with age in our countries, and in the colder regions many other animals without it....

Fourthly, while we so eagerly adhere unto antiquity and the accounts of elder times, we are to consider the fabulous condition thereof. And that we shall not deny if we call to mind the mendacity of Greece, from whom we have received most relations, and that a considerable part of ancient times was by the Greeks themselves termed μύθικον,[6] that is, made up or stuffed out with fables. And surely the fabulous inclination of those days was greater than any since, which swarmed so with fables and from such slender grounds took hints for fictions, poisoning the world ever after; wherein how far they exceeded may be exemplified by Palaephatus, in his book of *Fabulous Narrations*. That fable of Orpheus, who by the melody of his music made woods and trees to follow him, was raised upon a slender foundation; for there were a crew of mad women, retired unto a mountain from whence, being pacified by his music, they descended with boughs in their hands, which unto the fabulosity of those times proved a sufficient ground to celebrate unto all posterity the magic of Orpheus' harp and its power to attract the senseless trees about it. That Medea the famous sorceress could renew youth and make old men young again was nothing else but that from the knowledge of simples[7] she had a receipt to make white hair black and reduce old heads into the tincture of youth again.... 'Twas ground enough to fancy wings unto Daedalus, in that he stole out of a window from Minos and sailed away with his son Icarus; who steering his course wisely, escaped, but his son, carrying too high a sail, was drowned.

3] unsophisticated   4] of rustic matters   5] yoke-animals   6] myth
7] medicinal herbs

That Niobe[8] weeping over her children was turned into a stone was nothing else but that during her life she erected over their sepultures a marble tomb of her own. When Actaeon[9] had undone himself with dogs and the prodigal attendance of hunting, they made a solemn story how he was devoured by his hounds. And upon the like grounds was raised the anthropophagy[10] of Diomedes his horses. Upon as slender a foundation was built the fable of the Minotaur, for one Taurus, a servant of Minos, gat his mistress Pasiphae with child, from whence the infant was named Minotaurus. Now this unto the fabulosity of those times was thought sufficient to accuse Pasiphae of bestiality, or admitting conjunction with a bull, and in succeeding ages gave a hint of depravity unto Domitian to act the fable into reality.[11] In like manner, as Diodorus plainly delivereth, the famous fable of Charon[12] had its nativity; who being no other but the common ferry-man of Egypt that wafted over the dead bodies from Memphis,[13] was made by the Greeks to be the ferryman of hell, and solemn stories raised after of him. Lastly, we shall not need to enlarge if that be true which grounded the generation of Castor and Helen out of an egg because they were born and brought up in an upper room, according unto the word ωον,[14] which with the Lacadaemonians had also that signification....

Nor is only a resolved prostration unto antiquity a powerful enemy unto knowledge, but any confident adherence unto authority or resignation of our judgements upon the testimony of any age or author whatsoever.

For first, to speak generally, an argument from authority to wiser examinations is but a weaker kind of proof, it being but a topical probation, and, as we term it, an inartificial[15] argument, depending upon a naked asseveration; wherein neither declaring the causes, affections[16] or adjuncts of what we believe, it carrieth not with it the reasonable inducements of knowledge. And therefore *Contra negantem*

8] a queen of Thebes and proud mother of twelve children, who were slain at the command of the jealous Leto, Zeus' wife. Zeus turned Niobe to stone on Mt Sipylus.   9] a hunter who unluckily spied Diana bathing; Diana had his dogs devour him.   10] cannibalism   11] Domitian was notoriously sensual   12] the ferryman who conducted the dead over the river Styx and into the underworld   13] the major city and religious centre of Lower Egypt   14] two of Leda's children, from her union with Zeus. He appeared to her in the form of a swan, and the babies were said to have hatched from eggs (ωον).   15] artless, clumsy, natural   16] properties

principia,[17] *Ipse dixit*[18] or *Oportet discentem credere,*[19] although postulates very accommodable unto junior indoctrinations, yet are their authorities but temporary, and not to be embraced beyond the minority of our intellectuals[20]....

PE I.vi-vii.40-47

¶ Hieroglyphical errors

The hieroglyphical doctrine of the Egyptians (which in their four hundred years' cohabitation[1] some conjecture they learned from the Hebrews) hath much advanced many popular conceits. For using an alphabet of things and not of words, through the image and pictures thereof, they endeavoured to speak their hidden conceits in the letters and language of nature. In pursuit whereof, although in many things they exceeded not their true and real apprehensions,[2] yet in some other they either framing the story or taking up the tradition, conducible unto their intentions,[3] obliquely confirmed many falsities; which as authentic and conceded truths did after pass unto the Greeks, from them unto other nations, and are still retained by symbolical writers, emblematists, heralds, and others. Whereof some are strictly maintained for truths, as naturally making good their artificial representations;[4] others, symbolically intended, are literally received, and swallowed in the first sense, without all gust of the second;[5] whereby we pervert the profound and mysterious knowledge of Egypt containing the arcanas[6] of Greek antiquities, the key of many obscurities and ancient learning extant. Famous herein in former ages were Heraiscus, Cheremon, Epius, especially Orus Apollo Niliacus, who lived in the reign of Theodosius, and in Egyptian language left two books of hieroglyphics, translated into Greek by Philippus, and a large collection of all made after by Pierius. But no man is likely to profound[7] the ocean of that doctrine beyond that eminent example of industrious learning, Kircherus.

17] 'Against [one] who denies first principles [it is useless to argue]'   18] 'He said so himself' (implying that the assertion is arbitrary and unsupported) 19] 'The pupil ought to believe [what the teacher tells him]'   20] intellect

1] the captivity of the Israelites in Egypt   2] genuine understanding 3] adapting the tradition   4] characteristics falsely attributed to things having become accepted truths, they seem to confirm the hieroglyphical intentions of the emblematists   5] the literal sense overriding the symbolical one   6] the great alchemical or other secrets of nature   7] plumb

Painters, who are the visible representers of things, and such as by the learned sense of the eye endeavour to inform the understanding, are not inculpable herein, who, either describing naturals as they are or actions as they have been, have oftentimes erred in their delineations; which, being the books that all can read, are fruitful advancers of these conceptions, especially in common and popular apprehensions, who, being unable for farther enquiry, must rest in the draught and letter of their descriptions.

Lastly, poets and poetical writers have in this point exceeded others, trimly advancing the Egyptian notions of harpies, phoenix, griffins, and many more. Now, however, to make use of fictions, apologues[8] and fables be not unwarrantable, and the intent of these inventions might point at laudable ends, yet do they afford our junior capacities a frequent occasion of error, settling impressions in our tender memories which our advanced judgements generally neglect to expunge. This way the vain and idle fictions of the Gentiles did first insinuate into the heads of Christians; and thus are they continued even unto our days, our first and literary apprehensions being commonly instructed in authors which handle nothing else....

PE I.ix.61-2

¶ Errors in plant lore

Many molas[1] and false conceptions there are of mandrakes. The first, from great antiquity, conceiveth the root thereof resembleth the shape of man, which is a conceit not to be made out by ordinary inspection or any other eyes than such as regarding the clouds behold them in shapes conformable to preapprehensions.[2]

Now, whatever encouraged the first invention, there have not been wanting many ways of its promotion. The first, a catachrestical[3] and far-derived similitude it holds with man, that is, in a bifurcation or division of the root into two parts, which some are content to call thighs; whereas notwithstanding they are ofttimes three, and when but two, commonly so complicated and crossed that men for this deceit are fain to effect their design in other plants, and as fair a resemblance is often found in carrots, parsnips, briony, and many others.

8] moral tales

1] fleshy masses in the womb; false pregnancies   2] people see in clouds the shapes they wish to find   3] catachresis – the misuse of words

There are, I confess, divers plants which carry about them not only the shape of parts, but also of whole animals, but surely not all thereof unto whom this conformity is imputed. Whoever shall pursue the signatures of Crollius, or rather the *Phytognomy* of Porta, and strictly observe how vegetable realities are commonly forced into animal representations, may easily perceive in very many the semblance is but postulatory, and must have a more assimilating fancy than mine to make good many thereof.

PE II.vi.140

¶ Of the basilisk[1]

...Nor is only the existency of this animal considerable, but many things delivered thereof, particularly its poison and its generation. Concerning the first, according to the doctrine of the ancients men still affirm that it killeth at a distance, that it poisoneth by the eye and by priority of vision.[2] Now, that deleterious it may be at some distance, and destructive without corporal contaction, what uncertainty soever there be in the effect, there is no high improbability in the relation. For if plagues and pestilential atoms have been conveyed in the air from different regions, if men at a distance have infected each other, if the shadows of some trees be noxious,[3] if torpedoes[4] deliver their opium at a distance and stupefy beyond themselves, we cannot reasonably deny that (beside our gross and restrained poisons requiring contiguity[5] unto their actions) there may proceed from subtler seeds more agile emanations which contemn those laws and invade at distance unexpected.

That this venation[6] shooteth from the eye, and that this way a basilisk may empoison (although thus much be not agreed upon by authors, some imputing it unto the breath, others unto the bite) it is not a thing impossible. For eyes receive offensive impressions from their objects and may have influences destructive to each other. For the visible species of things strike not our senses immaterially,[7] but streaming in corporal rays[8] do carry with them the qualities of the object from whence they flow and the medium through which they

1] mythical beast hatched by a serpent from a cock's egg   2] glancing first
3] in *PE* II.7 Browne says that snakes cannot stand to be in the shadow of an ash tree   4] electric ray-fish   5] our less remarkable poisons require physical contact with their object   6] strike against prey   7] without physical cause or contact   8] physical rays

pass. Thus, through a green or red glass all things we behold appear of the same colours; thus, sore eyes affect those which are sound, and themselves also by reflection, as will happen to an inflamed eye that beholds itself long in a glass;[9] thus is fascination[10] made out, and thus also it is not impossible what is affirmed of this animal, the visible rays of their eyes carrying forth the subtlest portion of their poison, which, received by the eye of man or beast, infecteth first the brain and is from thence communicated unto the heart....

As for the generation of the basilisk, that it proceedeth from a cock's egg hatched under a toad or serpent, it is a conceit as monstrous as the brood itself. For if we should grant that cocks growing old and unable for emission amass within themselves some seminal matter which may after conglobate into the form of an egg, yet will this substance be unfruitful, as wanting one principle of generation and a commixture of both sexes, which is required unto production, as may be observed in the eggs of hens not trodden, and as we have made trial in some which are termed cocks' eggs.[11] It is not, indeed, impossible that from the sperm of a cock, hen, or other animal, being once in putrescence, either from incubation or otherwise, some generation may ensue; not univocal[12] and of the same species, but some imperfect or monstrous production, even as in the body of man from putrid humours and peculiar ways of corruption there have succeeded strange and unseconded[13] shapes of worms, whereof we have beheld some ourselves, and read of others in medical observations. And so may strange and venomous serpents be several ways engendered; but that this generation should be regular and alway produce a basilisk is beyond our affirmation, and we have good reason to doubt.

PE III.vii.176-7

¶Elephant errors

....of the elephant...there generally passeth an opinion it hath no joints; and this absurdity is seconded with another, that being unable to lie down, it sleepeth against a tree, which, the hunters observing, do saw it almost asunder, whereon the beast relying, by the fall of the tree falls also down itself and is able to rise no more; which conceit is not

9] the disease of an inflamed eye, by being reflected in a mirror, can cast the infection back into the other eye of the beholder   10] casting of spells, attractive influence   11] small, yolkless eggs   12] of similar parts   13]* unique

the daughter of later times but an old and grey-headed error even in the days of Aristotle, as he delivereth in his book, *De incessu animalium*,[1] and stands successively related by several other authors – by Diodorus Siculus, Strabo, Ambrose, Cassiodore, Solinus, and many more. Now herein methinks men much forget themselves, not well considering the absurdity of such assertions....

PE III.i.157

¶ Of the salamander

That a salamander is able to live in flames, to endure and put out fire, is an assertion not only of great antiquity but confirmed by frequent and not contemptible testimony. The Egyptians have drawn it into their hieroglyphics; Aristotle seemeth to embrace it; more plainly Nicander, Serenus Sammonicus, Aelian and Pliny, who assigns the cause of this effect: an animal (saith he) so cold that it extinguisheth the fire like ice. All which notwithstanding, there is on the negative authority and experience. Sextius, a physician, as Pliny delivereth, denied this effect; Dioscorides affirmed it a point of folly to believe it; Galen, that it endureth the fire a while, but in continuance is consumed therein. For experimental conviction, Mathiolus affirmeth he saw a salamander burnt in a very short time; and of the like assertion is Amatus Lusitanus; and most plainly Pierius, whose words in his *Hieroglyphics* are these: 'Whereas it is commonly said that a salamander extinguisheth fire, we have found by experience that it is so far from quenching hot coals that it dieth immediately therein.' As for the contrary assertion of Aristotle, it is but by hearsay, as common opinion believeth, *Haec enim (ut aiunt) ignem ingrediens, eum extinguit*;[1] and therefore there was no absurdity in Galen, when as a septical[2] medicine he commended the ashes of a salamander; and magicians, in vain from the power of this tradition, at the burning of towns or houses expect a relief from salamanders....

It hath been much promoted by stories of incombustible napkins and textures[3] which endure the fire, whose materials are called by the name of salamander's wool; which many, too literally apprehending,

1] 'On the Gaits of Animals'

1] 'Going into the fire she even (so they say) extinguishes it.'   2] a corruptive or putrefactive medicine, such as arsenic, which destroys what it touches   3] woven fabric

conceive some investing part, or tegument[4] of the salamander, wherein beside that they mistake the condition of this animal (which is a kind of lizard, a quadruped corticated[5] and depilous, that is, without wool, fur, or hair) they observe not the method and general rule of nature, whereby all quadrupeds oviparous,[6] as lizards, frogs, tortoise, chameleons, crocodiles, are without hair, and have no covering part or hairy investment[7] at all. And if they conceive that from the skin of the salamander these incremable pieces are composed, beside the experiments made upon the living, that of Brassavolus will step in, who in the search of this truth did burn the skin of one dead.

Nor is this salamander's wool desumed[8] from any animal, but a mineral substance, metaphorically so called from this received opinion ... that which the ancients named *Asbeston*, and Pancirollus treats of in the chapter of *Linum vivum*,[9] whereof by art were weaved napkins, shirts, and coats inconsumable by fire; and wherein in ancient times, to preserve their ashes pure, and without commixture, they burnt the bodies of kings....

PE III.xiv.202-04

¶ Hermaphrodite hares

The double sex of single hares, or that every hare is both male and female, beside that vulgar opinion, was the affirmative of Archelaus, of Plutarch, Philostratus, and many more. Of the same belief have been the Jewish rabbins.[1] The same is likewise confirmed from the Hebrew word which, as though there were no single males of that kind, hath only obtained a name of the feminine gender; as also from the symbolical foundation of its prohibition in the law[2] and what vices therein are figured; that is, not only pusillanimity and timidity from its temper, feneration[3] or usury from its fecundity and superfetation,[4] but from this mixture of sexes, unnatural venery[5] and degenerous effemination. Nor are there hardly any who either treat of mutation or mixtion of sexes who have not left some mention of this point, some speaking positively, others dubiously, and most resigning it unto the enquiry of

4] covering or skin   5] having bark-like skin   6] born from an egg
7] covering   8] taken from   9] living flax

1] rabbinical commentators on the Old Testament   2] Leviticus 11:5 and Deuteronomy 14:7 prohibit the eating of hares   3] usury (fig.)   4] additional and subsequent conception during pregnancy   5] sexual activity

the reader. Now hereof to speak distinctly, they must be male and female by mutation and succession of sexes; or else by composition,[6] mixture or union thereof.

As for the mutation of sexes or transition into one another, we cannot deny it in hares, it being observable in man. For hereof, beside Empedocles or Tiresias,[7] there are not a few examples; and though very few, or rather none which have emasculated or turned women, yet very many who from an esteem or reality of being women have infallibly proved men; some at the first point of their menstrous eruptions, some in the day of their marriage, others many years after, which occasioned disputes at law and contestations concerning a restore of the dowry. And that not only mankind but other animals may suffer this transsexion, we will not deny or hold it at all impossible, although I confess, by reason of the postic[8] and backward position of the feminine parts in quadrupeds, they can hardly admit the substitution of a protrusion, effectual unto masculine generation, except it be in retromingents[9] and such as couple backward....

Now the grounds that begat or much promoted the opinion of a double sex in hares, might be some little bags or tumours, at first glance representing stones or testicles, to be found in both sexes about the parts of generation which men, observing in either sex, were induced to believe a masculine sex in both. But to speak properly, these are no testicles or parts official unto generation, but glandulous substances that seem to hold the nature of emunctories.[10] For herein may be perceived slender perforations at which may be expressed a black and feculent matter. If therefore from these we shall conceive a mixtion of sexes in hares, with fairer reason we may conclude it in beavers, whereof both sexes contain a double bag or tumour in the groin, commonly called the cod of Castor,[11] ...

...The last foundation was retromingency, or pissing backward; for men observing both sexes to urine backward, or aversely between their legs, they might conceive there was a feminine part in both; wherein they are deceived by the ignorance of the just and proper site of the pizzel, or part designed unto the excretion of urine, which in the hare holds not the common position, but is aversely seated, and in its distention inclines unto the coccyx or scut. Now from the nature of this

6] composite nature   7] Empedocles' philosophy describes sexual generation as arising from universal bisexuality; Tiresias was a Theban soothsayer who was turned into a woman for a time by Hera   8] hind, back   9] animals who urinate backwards   10] excretory ducts in the body   11] excretory scent-glands of the beaver

position there ensueth a necessity of retrocopulation,[12] which also promoteth the conceit; for some, observing them to couple without ascension,[13] have not been able to judge of male or female or to determine the proper sex in either. And to speak generally, this way of copulation is not appropriate unto hares; nor is there one, but many ways of coition, according to divers shapes and different conformations. For some couple laterally or sidewise, as worms; some circularly or by complication, as serpents; some pronely, that is, by contaction of the ventral[14] parts in both, as apes, porcupines, hedgehogs, and such as are termed *Mollia*, as the cuttlefish and the purple;[15] some mixtly, that is, the male ascending the female, or by application of the ventral parts of the one unto the postic parts of the other, as most quadrupeds; some aversely, as all crustaceous animals, lobsters, shrimps, and crevisses,[16] and also retromingents, as panthers, tigers, and hares. This is the constant law of their coition; this they observe and transgress not. Only the vitiosity[17] of man hath acted the varieties hereof; nor content with a digression from sex or species, hath in his own kind run through the anomalies of venery; and been so bold not only to act, but represent to view, the irregular ways of lust.

PE III.xvii.212-19

¶ Of the picture of the pelican

And first, in every place we meet with the picture of the pelican opening her breast with her bill and feeding her young ones with the blood distilling from her. Thus is it set forth not only in common signs, but in the crest and scutcheon of many noble families; hath been asserted by many holy writers; and was an hieroglyphic of piety and pity among the Egyptians, on which consideration, they spared them at their tables.... Some ground hereof I confess we may allow, nor need we deny a remarkable affection in pelicans toward their young; for Aelian, discoursing of storks and their affection toward their brood whom they instruct to fly and unto whom they redeliver up the provision of their bellies, concludeth at last that herons and pelicans do the like.

As for the testimonies of ancient fathers and ecclesiastical writers, we may more safely conceive therein some emblematical than any real

12] backward copulation   13] in which the male mounts the female
14] abdominal   15] purple-fish, a mollusc which yields a purple dye
16] crayfish   17] defective nature; vices

story: so doth Eucherius confess it to be the emblem of Christ.[1] And we are unwilling literally to receive that account of Jerome, that perceiving her young ones destroyed by serpents she openeth her side with her bill by the blood whereof they revive and return unto life again; by which relation they might indeed illustrate the destruction of man by the old serpent and his restorement by the blood of Christ; and in this sense[2] we shall not dispute the like relations of Austin, Isidore, Albertus, and many more, and under an emblematical intention we accept it in coat-armour[3]....

And lastly, as concerning the picture, if naturally examined and not hieroglyphically conceived, it containeth many improprieties, disagreeing almost in all things from the true and proper description. For, whereas it is commonly set forth green or yellow, in its proper colour it is inclining to white, excepting the extremities or tops of the wing feathers, which are brown. It is described in the bigness of a hen, whereas it approacheth and sometimes exceedeth the magnitude of a swan. It is commonly painted with a short bill, whereas that of the pelican attaineth sometimes the length of two spans.[4] The bill is made acute or pointed at the end, whereas it is flat and broad, though somewhat inverted at the extreme. It is described like fissipedes, or birds which have their feet or claws divided, whereas it is palmipedous, or fin-footed like swans and geese, according to the method of nature in latirostrous or flat-billed birds, which being generally swimmers, the organ is wisely contrived unto the action, and they are framed with fins or oars upon their feet; and therefore they neither light, nor build on trees (if we except cormorants, who make their nests like herons). Lastly, there is one part omitted more remarkable than any other, that is, the jowl or crop adhering unto the lower side of the bill and so descending by the throat, a bag or satchel very observable and of a capacity almost beyond credit; which, notwithstanding, this animal could not want, for therein it receiveth oysters, cockles, scallops, and other testaceous animals, which being not able to break, it retains them until they open, and vomiting them up, takes out the meat contained. This is that part preserved for a rarity, and wherein (as Sanctius delivers) in one dissected a negro child was found.

A possibility there may be of opening and bleeding their breast, for this may be done by the uncous[5] and pointed extremity of their bill, and some probability also that they sometimes do it for their own

1] because it sheds its blood to feed its children   2] i.e. emblematical
3] coats of arms   4] about eighteen inches   5] curved

relief, though not for their young ones; that is, by nibbling and biting themselves on their itching part of their breast upon fullness or acrimony[6] of blood. And the same may be better made out, if (as some relate) their feathers on that part are sometimes observed to be red and tincted with blood.

PE V.i.338-40

¶ Dietary laws and habits

Why we confine our food unto certain animals and totally reject some others, how these distinctions crept into several nations and whether this practice be built upon solid reason, or chiefly supported by custom or opinion, may admit consideration.

For first, there is no absolute necessity to feed on any; and if we resist not the stream of authority, and several deductions from Holy Scripture, there was no sarcophagy[1] before the flood; and without the eating of flesh our fathers from vegetable aliments preserved themselves unto longer lives than their posterity by any other. For whereas it is plainly said, 'I have given you every herb which is upon the face of all the earth, and every tree, to you it shall be for meat;'[2] presently after the deluge, when the same had destroyed or infirmed the nature of vegetables, by an expression of enlargement it is again delivered, 'Every moving thing that liveth, shall be meat for you, even as the green herb, have I given you all things.'[3]

And therefore, although it be said that Abel was a shepherd, and it be not readily conceived the first men would keep sheep except they made food thereof, great expositors tell us that it was partly for their skins, wherewith they were clothed, partly for their milk, whereby they were sustained, and partly for sacrifices, which they also offered....

But whenever it be acknowledged that men began to feed on flesh, yet how they betook themselves after to particular kinds thereof, with rejection of many others, is a point not clearly determined. As from the distinction of clean and unclean beasts,[4] the original is obscure, and salveth[5] not our practice; for no animal is naturally unclean, or hath this character in nature; and therefore whether in this distinction there

6] bitter humour or fluid

1] eating of flesh   2] Genesis 1:29   3] Genesis 9:3   4] the distinction made in Leviticus 11 and Deuteronomy 14:3-19   5] explains

were not some mystical intention;[6] whether Moses, after the distinction made of unclean beasts, did not name these so before the flood by anticipation;[7] whether this distinction before the flood were not only in regard of sacrifices, as that delivered after was in regard of food (for many were clean for food which were unclean for sacrifice); or whether the denomination were but comparative, and of beasts less commodious for food although not simply bad, is not yet resolved....

And if we take a view of other nations we shall discover that they refrained many meats upon the like considerations. For in some the abstinence was symbolical: so Pythagoras enjoined abstinence from fish (that is, luxurious and dainty dishes); so, according to Herodotus, some Egyptians refrained from swine's flesh as an impure and sordid animal which whoever but touched, was fain to wash himself.

Some abstained superstitiously or upon religious consideration: so the Syrians refrained from fish and pigeons; the Egyptians of old, dogs, eels and crocodiles (though Leo Africanus delivers that many of late do eat them with good gust); and Herodotus also affirmeth that the Egyptians of elephantina (unto whom they were not sacred) did eat thereof in elder times, and writers testify that they are eaten at this day in India and America. And so, as Caesar reports, unto the ancient Britons it was piaculous[8] to taste a goose, which dish at present no table is without....

Moreover, while we single out several dishes and reject others, the selection seems but arbitrary, or upon opinion; for many are commended and cried up in one age which are decried and nauseated in another. Thus, in the days of Maecenas no flesh was preferred before young asses, which notwithstanding became abominable unto succeeding appetites. At the table of Heliogabalus the combs of cocks were an esteemed service, which country stomachs will not admit at ours. The sumen, or belly and dugs of swine with pig (and sometimes beaten and bruised unto death); the womb of the same animal, especially that was barren or else had cast her young ones, though a tough and membranous part, was magnified by Roman palates, whereunto nevertheless we cannot persuade our stomachs. How alec, muria, and garum[9] would humour our gust I know not; but surely few there are that could delight in their cyceon – that is, the common draught of honey, cheese, parched barley-flour, oil and wine – which notwith-

6] some symbolic meaning   7] the animals declared unclean for sacrifice before the flood were included by Moses in his list of the animals declared unclean for food (Leviticus 11:47)   8]* sinful   9] alec, fish sauce or brine; muria, a pickling brine; garum, a rich fish sauce

standing was a commended mixture and in high esteem among them....

Now whether it were not best to conform unto the simple diet of our forefathers; whether pure and simple waters were not more healthful than fermented liquors; whether there be not an ample sufficiency without all flesh in the food of honey, oil, and the several parts of milk, in the variety of grains, pulses, and sorts of fruits; since either bread or beverage may be made almost of all; whether nations have rightly confined unto several meats, or whether the common food of one country be not more agreeable unto another; how indistinctly all tempers apply unto the same, and how the diet of youth and old age is confounded, were considerations much concerning health, and might prolong our days, but must not this discourse.

PE III.xxv.245-51

¶ Of the canicular or dog days

....Nor do we hereby reject or condemn a sober and regulated astrology; we hold there is more truth therein than in astrologers – in some more than many allow, yet in none so much as some pretend. We deny not the influence of the stars, but often suspect the due application[1] thereof, for though we should affirm that all things were in all things, that heaven were but earth celestified, and earth but heaven terrestrified, or that each part above had an influence upon its divided affinity[2] below, yet how to single out these relations and duly to apply their actions is a work ofttimes to be effected by some revelation and cabala[3] from above rather than any philosophy or speculation here below. What power soever they have upon our bodies, it is not requisite they should destroy our reasons – that is, to make us rely on the strength of nature when she is least able to relieve us, and when we conceive the heaven against us to refuse the assistance of the earth created for us. This were to suffer from the mouth of the dog above[4] what others do from the teeth of dogs below; that is, to be afraid of their proper remedy and refuse to approach any water,[5] though that hath often proved a cure unto their disease. There is in wise men a power beyond the stars, and Ptolemy encourageth us that by foreknowledge we may evade their actions; for, being but universal

---

1] interpretation   2] the likeness of earthly and celestial things   3] secret,
esoteric doctrine   4] Sirius, the Dog Star   5] a symptom of rabies

causes,[6] they are determined by particular agents[7] which being inclined, not constrained,[8] contain within themselves the casting[9] act
and a power to command the conclusion.

PE IV.xiii.336-7

¶ Natural language

....That children committed unto the school of nature, without institution, would naturally speak the primitive[1] language of the world was
the opinion of ancient heathens, and continued since by Christians,
who will have it our Hebrew tongue as being the language of Adam.
That this were true were much to be desired, not only for the easy
attainment of that useful tongue, but to determine the true and primitive Hebrew. For whether the present Hebrew be the unconfounded
language of Babel and that which, remaining in Heber, was continued
by Abraham and his posterity, or rather the language of Phoenicia and
Canaan wherein he lived, some learned men, I perceive, do yet remain
unsatisfied. Although I confess probability stands fairest for the
former, nor are they without all reason who think that at the confusion
of tongues there was no constitution of a new speech in every family,
but a variation and permutation of the old, out of one common language raising several dialects, the primitive tongue remaining still entire. Which they who retained might make a shift to understand most
of the rest, by virtue whereof in those primitive times and greener
confusions Abraham and the family of Heber was able to converse
with the Chaldeans, to understand Mesopotamians, Canaanites,
Philistines, and Egyptians, whose several dialects he could reduce unto
the original and primitive tongue and so to be able to understand
them.

PE V.xxiii.393-4

....As for the Egyptians, they invented another way of trial; for ...
Psammitichus their king attempted this decision by a new and unknown experiment, bringing up two infants with goats, and where
they never heard the voice of man, concluding that to be the

6] the reasons of action in the cosmos (from Aristotle's doctrine of four causes)
7] the power which effects ends   8] tending toward but not compelled
9] decisive

1] the *ur*-language spoken in Eden

ERROR 55

ancientest nation, whose language they should first deliver. But herein
he forgot that speech was by instruction, not instinct; by imitation,
not by nature; that men do speak in some kind but like parrots and as
they are instructed, that is, in simple terms and words expressing the
open notions of things, which the second act of reason compoundeth
into propositions, and the last into syllogisms and forms of ratiocina-
tion.[2]

PE VI.i.400

¶ Divination

....A practice there is among us to determine doubtful matters by the
opening of a book and letting fall a staff; which notwithstanding are
ancient fragments of pagan divinations. The first, an imitation of *Sortes
Homericae* or *Virgilianae*,[1] drawing determinations from verses casually occuring. The same was practised by Severus, who entertained
ominous hopes[2] of the Empire from that verse in Vergil, *Tu regere
imperio populos, Romane, memento;*[3] and Gordianus, who reigned but
few days, was discouraged by another, that is, *Ostendunt terris hunc
tantum fata, nec ultra esse sinunt.*[4] Nor was this only performed in
heathen authors, but upon the sacred text of Scripture, as Gregorius
Turonensis hath left some account and as the practice of the Emperor
Heraclius, before his expedition into Asia Minor, is delivered by
Cedrenus.

As for the divination or decision from the staff, it is an augurial
relic[5] and the practice thereof is accused by God himself: 'My people
ask counsel at their stocks, and their staff declareth unto them.'[6] Of
this kind of rhabdomancy[7] was that practised by Nebuchadnezzar in
that Chaldean miscellany[8] delivered by Ezekiel: 'the King of Babylon
stood at the parting of the way, at the head of two ways to use divina-

2] devises logical propositions

1] bibliomancy or divination through books, especially those thought to be divinely inspired (here, Homer's and Vergil's): the book was allowed to fall open and
the revealed passage was interpreted for its prophetic content.   2] good hopes
3] 'Remember, Roman, to rule the nations by authority' (Anchises' words to
Aeneas, *Aeneid* Book VI)   4] 'The Fates reveal so much of him to the world but
permit nothing beyond to be revealed.' (Anchises to Aeneas, *Aeneid* Book VI)
5] the remains of an ancient mode of divination   6] Hosea 4:12
7] divination with a staff or wand; dowsing; Browne is using the term broadly to
include arrows   8] a mixture [of augurial methods]

tion, he made his arrows bright, he consulted with images, he looked in the liver; at the right hand were the divinations of Jerusalem.'⁹ That is, as Estius expounded it, the left way leading unto Rabbah, the chief city of the Ammonites, and the right into Jerusalem, he consulted idols and entrails,¹⁰ he threw up a bundle of arrows to see which way they would light; and falling on the right hand he marched towards Jerusalem. A like way of belomancy¹¹ or divination by arrows hath been in request with Scythians, Alanes, Germans, with the Africans and Turks of Algier. But of another nature was that which was prac-tised by Elisha, when by an arrow shot from an eastern window he presignified the destruction of Syria; or when according unto the three strokes of Joash, with an arrow upon the ground he foretold the number of his victories.¹² For thereby the spirit of God particulared¹³ the same, and determined the strokes of the king unto three, which the hopes of the prophet expected in twice that number.

PE V.xxiii.395-6

¶ Of sneezing

Concerning sternutation or sneezing, and the custom of saluting or blessing upon that motion, it is pretended, and generally believed to derive its original, from a disease wherein sternutation proved mortal, and such as sneezed, died. And this may seem to be proved from Carolus Sigonius, who in his *History of Italy* makes mention of a pes-tilence in the time of Gregory the Great that proved pernicious and deadly to those that sneezed; which notwithstanding will not suffi-ciently determine the grounds hereof, that custom having an elder era¹ than this chronology affordeth.

For although the age of Gregory extend above a thousand,² yet is this custom mentioned by Apuleius in the fable of the fuller's wife,³ who lived three hundred years before; by Pliny in that problem of his,

9] Ezekiel 21:21-2   10] haruspicy, the augurial practice based on the appear-ance of vital organs of animals (often sheep)   11]* divination by arrows   12] Joash, the King of Israel, smote the arrows three times, by which Elisha foretold he should be victorious three times over Syria (2 Kings 13:15-19)   13] mentioned particularly

1] an earlier origin   2] Pope Gregory the Great (?540-604) lived 1000 years before Browne   3] the woman who hid her lover from her husband in a wicker bleaching basket. His sneezes betrayed them, and the fumes killed him.(*Golden Ass* ix.25)

cur sternutantes salutantur,[4] and there are also reports that Tiberius the emperor, otherwise a very sour man, would perform this rite most punctually unto others, and expect the same from others unto himself.... There is also in the *Greek Anthology*[5] a remarkable mention hereof in an epigram upon one Proclus, the Latin whereof we shall deliver, as we find it often translated:

> *Non potis est Proclus digitis emungere nasum,*
> *Namque est pro nasi mole pusilla manus:*
> *Non vocat ille Jovem sternutans, quippe nec audit*
> *Sternutamentum, tam procul aure sonat.*

Proclus with his hand his nose can never wipe,
His hand too little is his nose to gripe;
He sneezing calls not Jove, for why? he hears
Himself not sneeze, the sound's so far from's ears.

Nor was this only an ancient custom among the Greeks and Romans and is still in force with us, but is received at this day in remotest parts of Africa. For so we read in Codignus, that upon a sneeze of the Emperor of Monomotapa[6] there passed acclamations successively through the city. And as remarkable an example there is of the same custom in the remotest parts of the east, recorded in the travels of Pinto.

But the history will run much higher if we should take in the rabbinical account hereof, that sneezing was a mortal sign even from the first man, until it was taken off by the special supplication of Jacob,[7] from whence, as a thankful acknowledgement, this salutation first began, and was after continued by the expression of *Tobim Chaiim* (or *vita bona*)[8] by standers by upon all occasion of sneezing....

The second way was superstitious and augurial, as Caelius Rhodiginus hath illustrated in testimonies as ancient as Theocritus and Homer; as appears from the Athenian master, who would have retired because a boatman sneezed; and the testimony of Austin that the ancients were wont to go to bed again if they sneezed while they put on their shoe. And in this way it was also of good and bad signification; so Aristotle hath a problem,[9] why sneezing from noon unto

---

4] why sneezings are blessed   5] the name given to a collection of several different anthologies of epigrammatic verse inscriptions written between about 100BC and AD100.   6] in what is now Zimbabwe   7] during his flight, Jacob prayed after a sneeze, thus preventing evil effects   8] 'to life'; 'Good life!'
9] a question proposed for academic discussion

midnight was good, but from night to noon unlucky? So Eustathius upon Homer observes that sneezing to the left hand was unlucky, but prosperous unto the right; so, as Plutarch relateth, when Themistocles sacrificed in his galley before the battle of Xerxes, and one of the assistants upon the right hand sneezed, Euphrantides the soothsayer presaged the victory of the Greeks and the overthrow of the Persians.

PE IV.ix.294-7

¶ Of the beginning of the world

....Others are so far from defining the original of the world or of mankind that they have held opinions not only repugnant unto chronology but philosophy – that is, that they had their beginning in the soil where they inhabited, assuming or receiving appellations conformable unto such conceits.[1] So did the Athenians term themselves αὐτόχθονες[2] or aborigines, and in testimony thereof did wear a golden insect[3] on their heads; the same name is also given unto the inlanders or midland inhabitants of this island by Caesar. But this is a conceit answerable unto the generation of the giants,[4] not admittable in philosophy, much less in divinity, which distinctly informeth we are all the seed of Adam, that the whole world perished unto eight persons before the flood, and was after peopled by the colonies of the sons of Noah. There was therefore never autochthon, or man arising from the earth, but Adam, for the woman, being formed out of the rib, was once removed from earth and framed from that element under incarnation.[5] And so although her production were not by copulation, yet was it in a manner seminal, for if in every part from whence the seed doth flow there be contained the idea[6] of the whole, there was a seminality and contracted Adam in the rib which by the information[7] of a soul was individuated into Eve. And therefore this conceit, applied unto the original of man and the beginning of the world, is more justly appropriable unto its end; for then indeed men shall rise out of the earth; the graves shall shoot up their concealed seeds, and in that great autumn men shall spring up and awake from their chaos again.

PE VI.i.399

1] the names they gave themselves reflect their beliefs about their origins
2] 'autochthons', self-generated from the earth   3] a cicada, said also to be born from the earth   4] Hesiod said that giants were born from the blood of Uranus which fell to earth   5] from what was already flesh   6] essence   7] formation within (the rib)

¶Of heliocentrism

....Now whether we adhere unto the hypothesis of Copernicus, affirming the earth to move and the sun to stand still; or whether we hold,
as some of late have concluded from the spots in the sun[1] which appear
and disappear again, that besides the revolution it maketh with its
orbs[2] it hath also a dinetical[3] motion and rolls upon its own poles;
whether, I say, we affirm these or no, the illations[4] before mentioned
are not thereby infringed. We therefore conclude this contemplation
and are not afraid to believe it may be literally said of the wisdom of
God what men will have but figuratively spoken of the works of Christ:
that if the wonders thereof were duly described, the whole world –
that is, all within the last circumference[5] – would not contain them.
For as his wisdom is infinite, so cannot the due expressions thereof be
finite; and if the world comprise him not, neither can it comprehend
the story of him.

PE VI.v.424

¶That there was no rainbow before the flood

That there shall no rainbow appear forty years before the end of the
world, and that the preceding drought unto that great flame shall
exhaust the materials[1] of this meteor[2] was an assertion grounded upon
no solid reason; but that there was not any in sixteen hundred years,
that is, before the flood, seems deducible from Holy Scripture, Gen. 9.
'I do set my bow in the clouds, and it shall be for a token of a Covenant
between me and the earth.' From whence notwithstanding we cannot
conclude the nonexistence of the rainbow; nor is that chronology
naturally established which computeth the antiquity of effects arising
from physical and settled causes by additional impositions from voluntary determinators.[3] Now by the decree of reason and philosophy the
rainbow hath its ground in nature, as caused by the rays of the sun
falling upon a roride[4] and opposite cloud; whereof some reflected,
others refracted, beget that semicircular variety we generally call the

1] described by several observers, including Galileo   2] orbit [around the earth]
3] rotary   4] deductions   5] the outermost sphere of the Ptolemaic universe

1] the drought will evaporate the necessary water   2] meteorological phenom-
enon   3] the era of certain natural events calculated by scholars using speculative
information   4] dew-laden

rainbow, which must succeed upon concurrence of causes and subjects aptly predisposed. And therefore to conceive there was no rainbow before because God chose this out as a token of the Covenant is to conclude the existence of things from their signalities,[5] or of what is objected unto the sense,[6] a coexistence with that which is internally presented unto the understanding. With equal reason we may infer there was no water before the institution of baptism, nor bread and wine before the Holy Eucharist....

... we shall not need to conceive God made the rainbow at this time if we consider that in its created and predisposed nature it was more proper for this signification than any other meteor or celestial appearancy whatsoever. Thunder and lightning had too much terror to have been tokens of mercy; comets or blazing stars appear too seldom to put us in mind of a covenant to be remembered often, and might rather signify the world should be once destroyed by fire, than never again by water. The galaxia or milky circle[7] had been more probable, for (beside that unto the latitude of thirty it becomes their horizon twice in four and twenty hours; and unto such as live under the equator in that space the whole circle appeareth) part thereof is visible unto any situation; but being only discoverable in the night and when the air is clear, it becomes of unfrequent and comfortless signification. A fixed star had not been visible unto all the globe, and so of too narrow a signality in a covenant concerning all. But rainbows are seen unto all the world and every position of sphere....

But the propriety of its election[8] most properly appeareth in the natural signification and prognostic of itself, as containing a mixed signality of rain and fair weather. For being in a roride cloud and ready to drop, it declareth a pluvious[9] disposure in the air; but because when it appears the sun must also shine, there can be no universal showers, and consequently no deluge. Thus when windows of the great deep were open, in vain men looked for the rainbow, for at that time it could not be seen which after appeared unto Noah. It might be therefore existent before the flood, and had in nature some ground of its addition.[10] Unto that of nature God superadded an assurance of his promise, that is, never to hinder its appearance, or so to replenish the heavens again as that we should behold it no more. And thus, without disparaging the promise, it might rain at the same time when God showed it unto Noah; thus was there more therein than the heathens

---

5] meanings　　6] makes no sense　　7] the Milky Way　　8] the symbolic aptness of the the rainbow　　9] rainy　　10] reason to exist

understood when they called it the *nuncia*[11] of the gods and the laugh
of weeping heaven; and thus may it be elegantly said, I put my bow,
not my arrow, in the clouds, that is, in the menace of rain and mercy
of fair weather.

Cabalistical[12] heads, who from that expression in Esay[13] do make a
book of heaven and read therein the great concernments of the earth,
do literally play on this, and from its semicircular figure resembling the
Hebrew letter] (caph), whereby is signified the uncomfortable
number of twenty, at which years Joseph was sold,[14] which Jacob lived
under Laban,[15] and at which men were to go to war,[16] do note a
propriety in its signification, as thereby declaring the dismal time of
the deluge. And Christian conceits do seem to strain as high while
from the irradiation of the sun upon a cloud they apprehend the mystery of the sun of righteousness in the obscurity of flesh; by the colours
green and red, the two destructions of the world by fire and water; or
by the colours of blood and water, the mysteries of baptism, and the
Holy Eucharist.

Laudable therefore is the custom of the Jews, who upon the appearance of the rainbow do magnify the fidelity of God in the memory
of His Covenant, according to that of Syracides ('Look upon the rainbow, and praise him that made it.')[17] And though some pious and
Christian pens have only symbolised the same from the mystery of its
colours, yet are there other affections[18] which might admit of theological allusions....

PE VII.iv.493-6

¶ Of the cessation of oracles

That oracles ceased or grew mute at the coming of Christ is best understood in a qualified sense and not without all latitude, as though
precisely there were none after, nor any decay before...After his death
we meet with many. Suetonius reports that the Oracle of Antium[1]

11] messenger   12] mystical interpreters of the Bible   13] 'And all the host
of heaven shall be dissolved, and the heavens shall be rolled together as a scroll...'
(Isaiah 34:4)   14] by his brothers to the Ishmeelites (Genesis 37:28)
15] Genesis 31:38,41   16] Numbers 1:3   17] Ecclesiasticus 43:11
18] attributes

1] Anzio

forewarned Caligula to beware of Cassius, who was one that conspired his death. Plutarch, enquiring why the oracles of Greece had ceased, excepteth that of Lebadia; and in the same place[2] Demetrius affirmeth the oracles of Mopsus and Amphilochus were much frequented in his days. In brief, histories are frequent in examples, and there want not some even to the reign of Julian.

What therefore may consist with history, by cessation of oracles with Montacutius we may understand their intercision, not abscission[3] or consummate desolation, their rare delivery, not total dereliction: and yet in regard of divers oracles we may speak strictly and say there was proper cessation. Thus may we reconcile the accounts of times and allow those few and broken divinations whereof we read in story and undeniable authors. For that they received this blow from Christ, and no other causes alleged by the heathens, from oraculous confession[4] they cannot deny; whereof upon record there are some very remarkable. The first, that oracle of Delphos[5] delivered unto Augustus:

> *Me puer Hebraeus Divos Deus ipse gubernans*
> *Cedere sede jubet, tristemque redire sub orcum;*
> *Aris ergo dehinc tacitus discedito nostris.*

> An Hebrew child, a god all gods excelling,
> To hell again commands me from this dwelling.
> Our altars leave in silence, and no more
> A resolution e'er from hence implore.

A second, recorded by Plutarch, of a voice that was heard to cry unto mariners at the sea, 'Great Pan is dead'[6] which is a relation very remarkable, and may be read in his *Defect of Oracles*. A third, reported by Eusebius in the life of his magnified Constantine, that about that time Apollo mourned, declaring his oracles were false and that the righteous upon earth did hinder him from speaking truth. And a fourth, related by Theodoret, and delivered by Apollo Daphnaeus unto Julian upon his Persian expedition, that he should remove the bodies about him before he could return an answer; and not long after his temple was burnt with lightning.

All which were evident and convincing acknowledgements of that power which shut his[7] lips and restrained that delusion which had

---

2] in Plutarch's *De defectu oraculorum*   3] intermission, not cutting off
4] from the admission of the oracles themselves   5] the premier oracle of Apollo
6] taken by Christians to refer to Christ's death and resurrection, which signalled
the death of the pagan gods   7] Satan's

reigned so many centuries. But as his malice is vigilant, and the sins of men do still continue a toleration of his mischiefs, he resteth not nor will he ever cease to circumvent the sons of the first deceived.[8] And therefore, expelled from oracles and solemn temples of delusion, he runs into corners, exercising minor trumperies, and acting his deceits in witches, magicians, diviners, and such inferior seducers. And yet (what is deplorable) while we apply ourselves thereto, and affirming that God hath left to speak by his prophets, except in doubtful matters a resolution from such spirits;[9] while we say the devil is mute yet confess that these can speak; while we deny the substance yet practise the effect, and in the denied solemnity maintain the equivalent efficacy;[10] in vain we cry that oracles are down: Apollo's altar still doth smoke, nor is the fire of Delphos out unto this day....

PE VII.xii.514-15

¶That Christ never laughed

....The same conceit[1] there passeth concerning our blessed Saviour, and is sometimes urged as an high example of gravity. And this is opinioned because in Holy Scripture it is recorded he sometimes wept but never that he laughed. Which howsoever granted, it will be hard to conceive how he passed his younger years and childhood without a smile if, as divinity affirmeth, for the assurance of his humanity unto men and the concealment of his divinity from the devil, he passed this age like other children, and so proceeded until he evidenced the same.[2] And surely herein no danger there is to affirm the act or performance of that whereof we acknowledge the power and essential property;[3] and whereby, indeed, he most nearly convinced the doubt of his humanity. Nor need we be afraid to ascribe that unto the incarnate Son which sometimes is attributed unto the uncarnate Father, of whom it is said, 'He that dwelleth in the heavens shall laugh the wicked to scorn.' For a laugh there is of contempt or indignation as well as of mirth and jocosity; and that our Saviour was not exempted from the ground hereof, that is, the passion of anger, regulated and rightly ordered by reason, the Schools do not deny; and besides, the experience

8] Adam and Eve   9] allow that in certain matters such 'inferior seducers' may provide answers   10] we hypocritically reject the rectitude of such prophesies, yet follow them none the less

1] that some men never laugh   2] his divinity   3] i.e. humanity

of the money-changers and dove-sellers in the temple is testified by St John, when he saith the speech of David[4] was fulfilled in our Saviour.

Now the alogy[5] of this opinion consisteth in the illation, it being not reasonable to conclude from Scripture negatively in points which are not matters of faith[6] and pertaining unto salvation. And therefore, although in the description of the creation there be no mention of fire, Christian philosophy did not think it reasonable presently to annihilate that element, or positively to decree there was no such thing at all. Thus, whereas in the brief narration of Moses there is no record of wine before the flood, we cannot satisfactorily conclude that Noah was the first that ever tasted thereof. And thus, because the word 'brain' is scarce mentioned once, but 'heart' above an hundred times in Holy Scripture, physicians that dispute the principality of parts are not from hence induced to bereave the animal organ[7] of its priority. Wherefore the Scriptures being serious, and commonly omitting such parergies,[8] it will be unreasonable from hence to condemn all laughter and from considerations inconsiderable to discipline a man out of his nature. For this is by a rustical severity[9] to banish all urbanity, whose harmless and confined condition, as it stands commended by morality, so is it consistent with religion and doth not offend divinity.

PE VII.xvi.529-30

¶Of the picture of the serpent tempting Eve

In the picture of paradise and delusion of our first parents, the serpent is often described with human visage (not unlike unto Cadmus or his wife in the act of their metamorphosis[1]), which is not a mere pictorial contrivance or invention of the picturer, but an ancient tradition and conceived reality as it stands delivered by Beda and authors of some antiquity; that is, that Satan appeared not unto Eve in the naked form of a serpent, but with a virgin's head, that thereby he might become more acceptable and his temptation find the easier entertainment;

4] 'The zeal of thine house hath eaten me up' (John 2:17)   5] absurdity
6] unless it were a matter of faith (which it is not), it would be foolish to assume that Christ never laughed simply because Scripture never mentions his laughing
7] the organ associated with the spirit (*anima*)   8]* a peripheral matter
9] unsubtle literal-mindedness

1] Cadmus, the founder of Thebes, and his wife, Harmony, were turned into serpents, having sown dragon's teeth to create men at the site of Thebes

which nevertheless is a conceit not to be admitted, and the plain and received figure is with better reason embraced.

For first, as Pierius observeth from Barcephas, the assumption of human shape had proved a disadvantage unto Satan, affording not only a suspicious amazement in Eve, before the fact, in beholding a third humanity beside herself and Adam, but leaving some excuse unto the woman which afterward the man took up with lesser reason; that is, to have been deceived by another like herself.

Again, there was no inconvenience in the shape assumed or any considerable impediment that might disturb that performance in the common form of a serpent. For whereas it is conceived the woman must needs be afraid thereof, and rather fly than approach it, it was not agreeable unto the condition of paradise and state of innocency therein if in that place, as most determine, no creature was hurtful or terrible unto man, and those destructive effects they now discover succeeded the curse and came in with thorns and briars.[2] And therefore Eugubinus (who affirmeth this serpent was a basilisk) incurreth no absurdity, nor need we infer that Eve should be destroyed immediately upon that vision; for noxious animals could offend them no more in the garden than Noah in the ark: as they peaceably received their names, so they friendly possessed their natures, and were their conditions destructive unto each other they were not so unto man, whose constitutions then were antidotes, and needed not fear poisons. And if (as most conceive) there were but two created of every kind, they could not at that time destroy either man or themselves, for this had frustrated the command of multiplication, destroyed a species, and imperfected the creation. And therefore also if Cain were the first man born, with him entered not only the act, but the first power of murther; for before that time neither could the serpent nor Adam destroy Eve, nor Adam and Eve each other, for that had overthrown the intention of the world and put its Creator to act the sixth day over again.

Moreover, whereas in regard of speech and vocal conference with Eve it may be thought he would rather assume an human shape and organs than the improper form of a serpent, it implies no material impediment, nor need we to wonder how he contrived a voice out of the mouth of a serpent, who hath done the like out of the belly of a pythonissa and the trunk of an oak, as he did for many years at Dodona.[3]

2] plants had no thorns or hurtful parts before the fall   3] Saul took counsel from a python inhabited by a spirit (I Chronicles 10:13); in the sanctuary of Zeus at Dodona, an oracle's voice spoke from a sacred oak

Lastly, whereas it might be conceived that an human shape was fitter for this enterprise – it being more than probable she would be amazed to hear a serpent speak – some conceive she might not yet be certain that only man was privileged with speech, and being in the novity[4] of the creation and inexperience of all things, might not be affrighted to hear a serpent speak. Beside, she might be ignorant of their natures, who was not versed in their names, as being not present at the general survey of animals when Adam assigned unto every one a name concordant unto its nature.[5]

PE V.iv.343-5

¶ Of the picture of Adam and Eve with navels

Another mistake there may be in the picture of our first parents, who after the manner of their posterity are both delineated with a navel. And this is observable not only in ordinary and stained[1] pieces, but in the authentic draughts of Urbin, Angelo and others; which notwithstanding cannot be allowed, except...what we deny unto nature we impute unto naturity[2] itself – that is, that in the first and most accomplished piece[3] the Creator affected superfluities or ordained parts without use or office....

And if we be led into conclusions that Adam had also this part, because we behold the same in ourselves, the inference is not reasonable, for if we conceive the way of his formation (or of the first animals) did carry in all points a strict conformity unto succeeding productions, we might fall into imaginations that Adam was made without teeth; or that he ran through those notable alterations in the vessels of the heart which the infant suffereth after birth. We need not dispute whether the egg or bird were first, and might conceive that dogs were created blind, because we observe they are littered so with us. Which to affirm is to confound, at least to regulate creation unto generation, the first acts of God unto the second of nature, which were determined in that general indulgence 'increase and multiply, produce or propagate each other' – that is, not answerable in all points, but in a prolonged method according to seminal progression.[4] For the for-

4] newness   5] Adam named the animals in Genesis 2:19-20; by tradition, their natures suggested their inherent names

1] stained glass   2]* the underlying creative power of nature   3] Adam
4] nature's method of propagation is not instantaneous, but observes the principles of growth and development

mation of things at first was different from their generation after, and although it had nothing to precede it, was aptly contrived for that which should succeed it. And therefore, though Adam were framed without this part (as having no other womb than that of his proper principles[5]), yet was not his posterity without the same, for the seminality of his fabric contained the power thereof,[6] and was endued with the science of those parts whose predestinations upon succession it did accomplish[7]....

They who hold the egg was before the bird prevent this doubt in many other animals, which also extendeth unto them; for birds are nourished by umbilical vessels and the navel is manifest sometimes a day or two after exclusion. The same is probable in oviparous exclusions, if the lesser part of eggs must serve for the formation, the greater part for nutriment. The same is made out in the eggs of snakes, and is not improbable in the generation of porwiggles or tadpoles, and may be also true in some vermiparous[8] exclusions, although (as we have observed in the daily progress in some) the whole maggot is little enough to make a fly without any part remaining.

PE V.v.345-7

¶Of the picture of Moses with horns

In many pieces, and some of ancient Bibles, Moses is described with horns. The same description we find in a silver medal: that is, upon one side Moses horned, and on the reverse the commandment against sculptile[1] images, which is conceived to be a coinage of some Jews in derision of Christians, who first began that portrait.[2]

The ground of this absurdity was surely a mistake of the Hebrew text in the history of Moses, when he descended from the Mount, upon the affinity of *kæren* and *karan*, that is, 'an horn', and 'to shine' (which is one quality of horn), the vulgar translation[3] conforming

---

5] the essence of his being with which he was endowed by God at his creation
6] within Adam was the ability to reproduce children who would follow the usual human pattern   7] in reproducing himself, he was inherently able to bestow those parts (e.g. a navel) on his offspring, even if he himself did not have them
8]* born in the form of larvae

1] graven (Exodus 20:4)   2] in derision of the Christian mistranslation of the Hebrew word 'to shine' in the Greek manuscripts, and of the subsequent pictorial tradition in the early church   3] the Vulgate or Latin Bible

unto the former: *Ignorabat quod cornuta esset facies eius. Qui videbant faciem Mosis esse cornutam.*[4] But the Chaldee paraphrase,[5] translated by Paulus Fagius, hath otherwise expressed it: *Moses nesciebat quod multus esset splendor gloriae vultus eius. Et viderunt filii Israel quod multa esset claritas gloriae faciei Mosis.*[6] The expression of the Septuagint is as large: δεδόξασται ἡ ὄψιζ τοῦ χρωματος τού προώπου – *Glorificatus est aspectus cutis, seu coloris faciei.*[7]

And this passage of the Old Testament is well explained by another of the New, wherein it is delivered that they could not steadfastly behold the face of Moses (διὰ τὴν δόξαν τοῦ προσωπου) – that is, for the glory of his countenance. And surely the exposition of one text is best performed by another, men vainly interposing their constructions where the Scripture decideth the controversy....

And therefore more allowable is the translation of Tremellius, *Quod splendida facta esset cutis faciei eius,*[8] or, as Estius hath interpreted it, *facies eius erat radiosa* (his face was radiant) and dispersing beams like many horns and cones about his head, which is also consonant unto the original signification and yet observed in the pieces of our Saviour and the Virgin Mary, who are commonly drawn with scintillations or radiant haloes about their head, which after the French expression[9] are usually termed the glory.

Now if, besides this occasional mistake, any man shall contend a propriety in this picture, and that no injury is done unto truth by this description because an horn is the hieroglyphic of authority, power and dignity, and in this metaphor is often used in Scripture, the piece, I confess, in this acception[10] is harmless and agreeable unto Moses; and under emblematical constructions we find that Alexander the Great and Attila king of the Huns in ancient medals are described with horns. But if from the common mistake or any solary consideration[11] we persist in this description, we vilify[12] the mystery of the irradiation[13] and authorise a dangerous piece conformable unto that of Jupiter

4] 'He knew not that his face was horned. They saw the face of Moses to be horned.' (Exodus 34:29)   5] the Babylonian version   6] 'Moses knew the splendor of his face's halo to be great. And the children of Israel saw that the halo of Moses' form was bright.'   7] 'On the one hand, the appearance of his person is full of glory, as, on the other, is the lustre of his face.'   8] 'What a splendid thing was the skin of his face'   9] from *gloire*, halo   10] under this interpretation   11] explanation implicating the sun   12] disparage   13] the mystery of halos

Hammon,[14] which was the sun, and therefore described with horns, as is delivered by Macrobius (*Hammonem quem Deum solem occidentem Lybies existimant, arietinis cornibus fingunt, quibus id animal valet, sicut radiis sol*).[15] We herein also imitate the picture of Pan,[16] and pagan emblem of nature. And if (as Macrobius and very good authors concede) Bacchus[17] (who is also described with horns) be the same deity with the sun, and if (as Vossius well contendeth) Moses and Bacchus were the same person, their descriptions must be relative,[18] or the tauricornous[19] picture of the one perhaps the same with the other.

PE V.ix.357-8

14] a conflation of the Egyptian Amoun and the Greek Zeus (or Jupiter). Jupiter Hammon was originally a god of shepherds (hence the symbolism of horns), and latterly was worshiped as the universal life-force (hence, perhaps, the connection with the sun)   15] 'The Lybians reckon their god Hammon to be the setting sun, and they portray him with ram's horns, since these are the source of that animal's strength, as sunbeams are of the sun's.'   16] also a pastoral and a universal god   17] a god of fertility depicted as a bull   18] one must arise from the other   19] with bull's horns

III. ANTIQUARIANISM

¶ On a bone dug from a cliff (to William Dugdale)

[Oct, 1660]

Sir,

I cannot sufficiently admire the ingenuous industry of Sir Robert
Cotton in preserving so many things of rarity and observation, nor
commend your own enquiries for the satisfaction of such particulars.
The petrified bone you sent me, which, with divers others, was found
underground near Connington, seems to be the vertebra, spondile or
rackbone of some large fish, and no terrestrious animal, as some upon
sight conceived as either of camel, rhinoceros, or elephant, for it is not
perforated and hollow, but solid, according to the spine of fishes, in
whom the spinal marrow runs in a channel above these solid racks or
spondiles.

It seems much too big for the largest dolphins, porpoises, or
swordfishes, and too little for a true or grown whale, but may be the
bone of some big cetaceous animal, as particularly of that which sea-
men call a grampus,[1] a kind of small whale, whereof some come short,
some exceed, twenty foot. And not only whales, but grampuses have
been taken in this estuary or mouth of the fenland rivers; and about
twenty years ago four were ran ashore near Hunstanton, and two had
young ones after they came to land.

But whether this fish were of the longitude of twenty foot (as is
conceived) some doubt may be made. For this bone containeth little
more than an inch in thickness, and not three inches in breadth, so
that it must have a greater number thereof than is easily allowable to
make out that longitude. For of the whale which was cast upon our
coast about six years ago, a vertebra or rackbone still preserved
containeth a foot in breadth, and nine inches in depth, yet the whale
with all advantages but sixty-two foot in length.

1] a class of spouting, blunt-headed whales

We are not ready to believe that wherever such relics of fish or sea animals are found the sea hath had its course. And Goropius Becanus long ago could not digest that conceit when he found great numbers of shells upon the highest Alps. For many may be brought unto places where they were not first found. Some bones of our whale were left in several fields, which when the earth hath obscured them may deceive some hereafter that the sea hath come so high. In the northern nations, where men live in houses of fish bones, and in the land of the ichthyophagi[2] near the Red Sea, where mortars were made of the backbones of whales, doors of their jaws, and arches of their ribs, when time had covered them they might confound after discoverers....It is not impossible that many such relics may yet remain in petrified substances from the deluge, as I have elsewhere declared. The greatest antiquities of mortal bodies may remain in petrified bones, whereof some may be older than the pyramids, in the petrified relics of the general inundation. But these being found in this place will not cause such doubts, but may afford conjecture that great waters have been where this was found, or at least drawn ashore. Herodotus and Plutarch thought it no small argument, from multitude of several shells found upon the higher ground of Egypt, to infer that those parts had been sometimes underwater....

For many years great doubt was made concerning those large bones found in some parts of England, and named giants' bones, till men considered they might be the bones of elephants[3] brought into this island by Claudius, and perhaps also by some succeeding emperors. In Brabant it caused no small amazement when the bones of three elephants were digged up, till wiser enquirers considered they might be brought hither by the tyrant Posthumus, or Saloninus, the son of Galienus. About Perugia many elephants' bones were found, which they resolve to be those which Hannibal brought into Italy. And such as are found in Campania and the more eastern parts may be those brought over by Pyrrhus.

But many things prove obscure in subterraneous discovery. The great golden horn found underground in Denmark graved with *imagini*[4] much perplexed the learned men of that country. In some chalk pits about Norwich many stags' horns are found, of large beams and branches, the solid parts converted into a chalky and fragile substance, the pithy part sometimes hollow and full of brittle earth and

2] fish-eaters   3] probably prehistoric mammoth remains   4] Wormius describes a great hunting horn, heavily decorated in gold with human figures, found in 1639

clay. In a churchyard of this city an oaken billet[5] was found in a coffin. About five years ago an humorous[6] man of this country, after his death and according to his own desire, was wrapped up in the horned hide of an ox, and so buried. Now when the memory hereof is past, how this may hereafter confound the discoverers, and what conjectures may arise thereof, it is not easy to conjecture.

Sir,

your servant to my power,

Tho. Browne

Letters 322-5

¶On Dr Dee's son (to Elias Ashmole)

[March, 1674]
I was very well acquainted with Dr Arthur Dee, and at one time or other he hath given me some account of the whole course of his life; he gave me a catalogue of what his father, Dr John Dee, had writ, and what he intended to write, but I think I have seen the same in some of his printed books, and that catalogue he gave me in writing I cannot yet find. I never heard him say one word of the book of spirits set out by Dr Casaubon, which if he had known, I make no doubt but he would have spoke of it unto me. For he was very inquisitive after any manuscripts of his father's, and desirous to print as many as he could possibly obtain....I have heard the Doctor say that he lived in Bohemia with his father both at Prague and other parts of Bohemia, that Prince or Count Rosenberg was their great patron, who delighted much in alchemy. I have often heard him affirm, and sometimes with oaths, that he had seen projection[1] made and transmutation of pewter dishes and flagons into silver, which the goldsmiths at Prague bought of them; and that Count Rosenberg played at quoits with silver quoits made by projection as before; that this transmutation was made by a powder they had, which was found in some old place, and a book lying by it containing nothing but hieroglyphs, which book his father bestowed much time upon; but I could not hear that he could make it out. He said also that Kelley dealt not justly by his father, and that he went away with the greatest part of the powder and was afterward imprisoned by the Emperor in a castle, from whence, attempting an escape down the wall, he fell and broke his leg and was imprisoned

5] a thick stick   6] eccentric

1] transmutation of base metals into precious ones

again. That his father Dr John Dee presented Queen Elizabeth with a little of the powder, who, having made a trial thereof, attempted to get Kelley out of prison and sent some to that purpose who, giving opium in drink unto the keepers, laid them so fast asleep that Kelley found opportunity to attempt an escape, and there were horses ready to carry him away, but the business unhappily succeeded as is before declared. He said that his father was in good credit with the Emperor Rudolphus, I think, and that he gave him some addition unto his coat of arms,[2] by a mathematical figure added, which I think may be seen at Mr Rowland Dee's house who had the picture and coat of arms of Dr John Dee which Dr Arthur Dee left at Mr Toley's when he died. Dr Arthur Dee was a young man when he saw this projection made in Bohemia, but he was so inflamed therewith that he fell early upon that study and read not much all his life but books of that subject....

Letters 296-7

¶ *Hydriotaphia: Urn-Burial, or, A Brief Discourse of the Sepulchral Urns Lately Found in Norfolk*

To my worthy and honoured Friend, Thomas Le Gros of Crostwick, Esquire

When the funeral pyre was out and the last valediction over, men took a lasting adieu of their interred friends, little expecting the curiosity of future ages should comment upon their ashes; and having no old experience of the duration of their relics, held no opinion of such after-considerations.

But who knows the fate of his bones, or how often he is to be buried? Who hath the oracle[1] of his ashes, or whither they are to be scattered? The relics of many lie like the ruins of Pompey's,[2] in all parts of the earth; and when they arrive at your hands these[3] may seem to have wandered far, who in a direct[4] and meridian travel have but few miles of known earth between yourself and the pole.

That the bones of Theseus should be seen again in Athens,[5] was not

2] granted him permission to add a figure to his arms

1] foreknowledge of their fate   2] 'although the earth of Asia and Europe covers the sons of Pompey, he himself is covered by that of Africa' (Martial)
3] the urns which are to be the subject of the essay   4] 'Little directly, but Sea between your house and Greenland'   5] the bones of Theseus, who had died on the island of Scyros, were retrieved

beyond conjecture and hopeful expectation; but that these should
arise so opportunely to serve yourself was an hit of fate, and honour
beyond prediction.

We cannot but wish these urns might have the effect of theatrical
vessels and great hippodrome urns[6] in Rome, to resound the
acclamations and honour due unto you. But these are sad and sepulchral pitchers which have no joyful voices, silently expressing old
mortality, the ruins of forgotten times, and can only speak with life
how long in this corruptible frame some parts may be uncorrupted, yet
able to outlast bones long unborn and noblest pile among us.

We present not these as any strange sight or spectacle unknown to
your eyes who have beheld the best of urns and noblest variety of
ashes, who are yourself no slender[7] master of antiquities, and can daily
command the view of so many imperial faces[8] – which raiseth your
thoughts unto old things and consideration of times before you when
even living men were antiquities;[9] when the living might exceed the
dead,[10] and to depart this world could not be properly said to go unto
the greater number – and so run up your thoughts upon the ancient of
days,[11] the antiquary's truest object, unto whom the eldest parcels are
young and earth itself an infant, and without Egyptian account[12]
makes but small noise in thousands.[13]

We were hinted by the occasion, not catched[14] the opportunity to
write of old things or intrude upon the antiquary. We are coldly
drawn[15] unto discourses of antiquities, who have scarce time before us
to comprehend new things or make out learned novelties. But seeing
they arose as they lay, almost in silence among us, at least in short
account suddenly passed over,[16] we were very unwilling they should
die again and be buried twice among us.[17]

Beside, to preserve the living and make the dead to live, to keep
men out of their urns and discourse of human fragments in them is not
impertinent to our profession,[18] whose study is life and death, who
daily behold examples of mortality, and of all men least need artificial

6] 'The great urns in the Hippodrome at Rome conceived to resound the voices of
people at their shows'   7] minor   8] on Roman coins in his collection
9] when men lived to great ages, especially in the antediluvian period recorded in
Genesis   10] when the world was so young that fewer people had already died
than were at present alive   11] God   12] the Egyptians estimated the final
age of the world as between 10,000 and 100,000 years; the western tradition
allowed 6,000   13] whatever the estimated age of the earth, it is as nothing to
the Almighty   14] did not seek out   15] reluctantly attracted   16] given
only cursory notice and description   17] return to oblivion again by being
unnoticed   18] that of doctor

mementoes or coffins by our bedside[19] to mind us of our graves.

'Tis time to observe occurrences and let nothing remarkable escape us. The supinity of elder days[20] hath left so much in silence, or time hath so martyred the records, that the most industrious heads do find no easy work to erect a new *Britannia*.[21]

'Tis opportune to look back upon old times and contemplate our forefathers. Great examples grow thin, and to be fetched from the past world. Simplicity flies away, and iniquity comes at long strides upon us. We have enough to do to make up ourselves[22] from present and past times, and the whole stage of things scarce serveth for our instruction. A complete piece of virtue must be made up from the centos[23] of all ages, as all the beauties of Greece could make but one handsome Venus.[24]

When the bones of King Arthur were digged up,[25] the old race[26] might think they beheld therein some originals of themselves. Unto these[27] of our urns, none here can pretend relation, and can only behold the relics of those persons who in their life giving the law unto their predecessors, after long obscurity now lie at their mercies. But remembering the early civility they brought upon these countries,[28] and forgetting long-past mischiefs, we mercifully preserve their bones and piss not upon their ashes.

In the offer of these antiquities we drive not at ancient families, so long out-lasted by them; we are far from erecting your worth upon the pillars of your forefathers,[29] whose merits you illustrate. We honour your old virtues, conformable unto times before you, which are the noblest armoury.[30] And having long experience of your friendly conversation, void of empty formality, full of freedom, constant and generous honesty, I look upon you as a gem of the old rock,[31] and must profess myself even to urns and ashes

Your ever faithful friend, and servant,
Thomas Browne
Norwich May 1 [1658]

19] a kind of *memento mori*, or reminder of the inevitability of death, affected by some in this period   20] laziness in recording events   21] William Camden's magisterial *Britannia* (1586-1607), one of the first works of historical scholarship to recognize the need of a reliable *British* history   22] select models for ourselves   23] patchworks   24] Zeuxis had to use the five most beautiful women of Croton to make a composite model for his picture of Helen 25] Camden reports that this was done in Somerset in the reign of Henry II 26] the pre-Noachics   27] the bones   28] the countries of the British Isles; Browne concludes that the urns are Roman   29] making your worthiness an example of the greatness of your ancestors   30] coats of arms (i.e. signs of gentility)   31] 'The best diamond comes from ancient rock'

¶ *Urn-Burial* Chapter I

In the deep discovery of the subterranean world, a shallow part would satisfy some enquirers who, if two or three yards were open about the surface, would not care to rake the bowels of Potosi[1] and regions towards the centre. Nature hath furnished one part of the earth and man another: the treasures of time lie high in urns, coins, and monuments scarce below the roots of some vegetables. Time hath endless rarities and shows of all varieties, which reveals old things in heaven, makes new discoveries in earth, and even earth itself a discovery. That great antiquity America lay buried for thousands of years, and a large part of the earth is still in the urn unto us.

Though if Adam were made out of an extract of the earth, all parts might challenge a restitution,[2] yet few have returned their bones far lower than they might receive them; not affecting the graves of giants, under hilly and heavy coverings, but, content with less than their own depth, have wished their bones might lie soft, and the earth be light upon them. Even such as hope to rise again would not be content with central interment,[3] or so desperately to place their relics as to lie beyond discovery and in no way to be seen again; which happy contrivance hath made communication with[4] our forefathers, and left unto our view some parts which they never beheld themselves.

Though earth hath engrossed the name,[5] yet water hath proved the smartest[6] grave, which in forty days swallowed almost mankind and the living creation, fishes not wholly escaping, except[7] the salt ocean were handsomely contempered[8] by admixture of the fresh element.

Many have taken voluminous pains to determine the state of the soul upon disunion, but men have been most fantastical in the singular contrivances of their corporal dissolution; whilst the soberest nations have rested in two ways, of simple inhumation and burning.

That carnal interment or burying was of the elder date, the old examples of Abraham and the Patriarchs are sufficient to illustrate, and were without competition[9] if it could be made out that Adam was buried near Damascus or Mount Calvary, according to some tradition. God himself, that buried but one,[10] was pleased to make choice of this

1] a silver-rich mountain in Peru   2] since Adam was said to have been made from dust from the four quarters of the earth, each of these quarters might ask for his (and our) dust back again at death   3] perhaps at the centre of the earth   4] offers insight into   5] 'interment', from *terra*   6] most effective   7] unless   8] moderated   9] exception   10] God is said to have buried Moses in the land of Moab (Deuteronomy 34:6)

way, collectible from expression and the hot contest between Satan and the Archangel about discovering the body of Moses.[11] But the practice of burning was also of great antiquity, and of no slender extent. For (not to derive the same from Hercules)[12] noble descriptions there are hereof in the Grecian funerals of Homer, in the formal obsequies of Patroclus and Achilles; and somewhat elder in the Theban war, and solemn combustion of Menoeceus and Archemorus, contemporary unto Jair, the eighth judge of Israel. Confirmable also among the Trojans from the funeral pyre of Hector, burnt before the gates of Troy, and the burning of Penthisilea, the Amazonian queen; and long continuance of that practice, in the inward countries of Asia; while as low as the reign of Julian we find that the King of Chionia burnt the body of his son and interred the ashes in a silver urn.

The same practice also extended far west, and besides Herulians, Getes, and Thracians,[13] was in use with most of the Celtae, Sarmatians,[14] Germans, Gauls, Danes, Swedes, Norwegians, not to omit some use thereof among Carthaginians and Americans, of greater antiquity among the Romans than most opinion, or Pliny seems to allow. For (beside the Old Table Laws[15] of burning or burying within the city, of making the funeral fire with planed wood, or quenching the fire with wine) Manlius the Consul burnt the body of his son; Numa by special clause of his will was not burnt but buried; and Remus was solemnly burned, according to the description of Ovid.

Cornelius Sylla was not the first whose body was burned in Rome, but of the Cornelian family, which being indifferently, not frequently, used before, from that time spread and became the prevalent practice. Not totally pursued in the highest run of cremation, for when even crows were funerally burnt, Poppaea the wife of Nero found a peculiar grave interment.[16] Now as all customs were founded upon some bottom of reason, so there wanted not grounds for this according to several apprehensions of the most rational dissolution. Some, being of the opinion of Thales, that water was the original of all things, thought it most equal to submit unto the principle of putrefaction, and con-

11] 'no man knoweth his sepulchre unto this day' (Deuteronomy 34:6); but Michael the Archangel and Satan had a dispute about the burying-place of Moses (Jude, 9)   12] reputed to have cremated a warrior named Argeus   13] tribes of the Balkan Peninsula and eastern Europe   14] tribes of Romania and the Ukraine   15] a set of fifth-century Roman laws   16] the Jewish wife of Nero, Poppaea was embalmed and buried in a mausoleum, in conformity with Jewish custom

clude in a moist relentment.[17] Others conceived it most natural to end
in fire, as due unto the master principle in the composition, according
to the doctrine of Heraclitus, and therefore heaped up large piles,
more actively to waft them toward that element, whereby they also
declined a visible degeneration into worms, and left a lasting parcel of
their composition.

Some apprehended a purifying virtue in fire, refining the grosser
commixture and firing out the ethereal particles[18] so deeply immersed
in it. And such as by tradition or rational conjecture held any hint of
the final pyre of all things, or that this element at last must be too hard
for all the rest, might conceive most naturally of the fiery dissolution.[19]
Others, pretending no natural grounds, politicly declined the malice
of enemies upon their buried bodies, which consideration led Sylla
unto this practice, who, having thus served the body of Marius, could
not but fear a retaliation upon his own, entertained[20] after in the civil
wars and revengeful contentions of Rome.

But as many nations embraced, and many left it indifferent, so others too much affected, or strictly declined this practice. The Indian
Brahmins seemed too great friends unto fire, who burnt themselves
alive and thought it the noblest way, to end their days in fire, according to the expression of the Indian, burning himself at Athens, in his
last words upon the pyre unto the amazed spectators, 'Thus I make
myself immortal.'

But the Chaldeans, the great idolators of fire, abhorred the burning
of their carcasses as a pollution of that deity.[21] The Persian magi declined upon the like scruple, and being only solicitous about their
bones, exposed their flesh to the prey of birds and dogs. And the
Parsees[22] now in India, which expose their bodies unto vultures, and
endure not so much as *feretra* or biers of wood, the proper fuel of fire,
are led on with such niceties. But whether the ancient Germans who
burned their dead held any such fear to pollute their deity of Herthus,
or the earth, we have no authentic conjecture.

The Egyptians were afraid of fire, not as a deity, but a devouring
element mercilessly consuming their bodies and leaving too little of
them; and therefore by precious embalmments, depositure in dry
earths, or handsome enclosure in glasses, contrived the notablest ways
of integral conservation.[23] And from such Egyptian scruples imbibed

17] softening (i.e. dissolution)   18] the impalpable spirit-substance in the
body   19] cremation   20] carried out   21] fire   22] Zoroastrian Persians   23] preservation of the whole body

by Pythagoras, it may be conjectured that Numa and the Pythagorical sect[24] first waived the fiery solution.

The Scythians, who swore by wind and sword, that is, by life and death, were so far from burning their bodies, that they declined all interment, and made their graves in the air;[25] and the ichthyophagi or fish-eating nations about Egypt affected the sea for their grave, thereby declining visible corruption and restoring the debt of their bodies; whereas the old heroes in Homer dread nothing more than water or drowning – probably upon the old opinion of the fiery substance of the soul, only extinguishable by that element – and therefore the poet emphatically implieth the total destruction in this kind of death, which happened to Ajax Oileus.

The old Balearians had a peculiar mode, for they used great urns and much wood but no fire in their burials, while they bruised the flesh and bones of the dead, crowded then into urns, and laid heaps of wood upon them. And the Chinois, without cremation or urnal interment of their bodies, make use of trees and much burning, while they plant a pine-tree by their grave, and burn great numbers of printed draughts[26] of slaves and horses over it, civilly content with their companies in effigy, which barbarous nations exact unto reality.

Christians abhorred this way of obsequies, and though they sticked not to give their bodies to be burnt in their lives, detested that mode after death, affecting rather a depositure than absumption,[27] and properly submitting unto the sentence of God to return not unto ashes but unto dust again, conformable unto the practice of the Patriarchs, the interment of our Saviour, of Peter, Paul, and the ancient martyrs, and so far at last declining promiscuous[28] interment with pagans, that some have suffered ecclesiastical censures for making no scruple thereof.

The Musselman believers will never admit this fiery resolution, for they hold a present[29] trial from their black and white angels in the grave, which they must have made so hollow that they may rise upon their knees.

The Jewish nation, though they entertained the old way of inhumation, yet sometimes admitted this practice, for the men of Jabesh burnt the body of Saul, and by no prohibited practice, to avoid contagion or pollution in time of pestilence, burnt the bodies of their friends.[30] And when they burnt not their dead bodies, yet sometimes

24] believing in the transmigration of souls after death   25] perhaps left their bodies uncovered   26] pictures   27]* wasting away [by fire]
28] undiscriminating   29] immediate   30] Amos 6:10

used great burnings near and about them, deducible from the expressions concerning Jehoram, Sedechias, and the sumptuous pyre of Asa,[31] and were so little averse from pagan burning that the Jews lamenting the death of Caesar, their friend and revenger on Pompey, frequented the place where his body was burnt for many nights together. And as they raised the noble monuments and mausoleums for their own nation, so they were not scrupulous in erecting some for others according to the practice of Daniel, who left that lasting sepulchral pile in Echbatana for the Medean and Persian kings.

But even in times of subjection and hottest use[32] they conformed not unto the Roman practice of burning; whereby the prophecy was secured concerning the body of Christ,[33] that it should not see corruption, or a bone should not be broken; which we believe was also providentially prevented, from the soldier's spear and nails that passed by the little bones both in his hands and feet, nor of ordinary contrivance, that it should not corrupt on the cross, according to the laws of Roman crucifixion, or an hair of his head perish, though observable in Jewish customs to cut the hairs of malefactors.

Nor in their long cohabitation with Egyptians crept into a custom of their exact embalming, wherein deeply slashing the muscles and taking out the brains and entrails, they had broken the subject of so entire a resurrection,[34] nor fully answered the types of Enoch, Eliah, or Jonah,[35] which yet to prevent or restore, was of equal facility unto that rising power, able to break the fasciations[36] and bands of death, to get clear out of the cerecloth, and an hundred pounds of ointment, and out of the sepulchre before the stone was rolled from it.[37]

But though they embraced not this practice of burning, yet entertained they many ceremonies agreeable unto Greek and Roman obsequies. And he that observeth their funeral feasts, their lamentations at the grave, their music, and weeping mourners, how they closed the eyes of their friends, how they washed, annointed, and kissed the dead, may easily conclude these were not mere pagan civilities. But whether

---

31] Zedechias (Jeremiah 34:5) and Asa (II Chronicles 16:14) were buried; Jehoram, for his wickedness, was denied this rite (II Chronicles 21:19)
32] most violent treatment   33] that His body should not see corruption was predicted in Psalm 16 and in Acts 2:31; that no bone should be broken, in John 19:36; and that no hair of the Apostles' heads should perish, by Christ himself in Luke 21:18   34] a resurrection of the intact body   35] who ascended whole into heaven   36] bandages   37] despite their elaborate embalming customs, the Egyptian dead could nevertheless rise from the grave as easily as the Old Testament figures whose bodies were not subject to the same treatment

that mournful burthen,[38] and treble calling out after Absalom,[39] had any reference unto the last conclamation and triple valediction used by other nations, we hold but a wavering conjecture.

Civilians make sepulture but of the law of nations,[40] others do naturally found it[41] and discover it also in animals. They that are so thick-skinned as still to credit the story of the phoenix may say something for animal burning; more serious conjectures find some examples of sepulture in elephants, cranes, the sepulchral cells of pismires and practice of bees, which civil society carrieth out their dead, and hath exequies,[42] if not interments.

¶ *Urn-Burial* Chapter II

The solemnities, ceremonies, rites of their cremation or interment, so solemnly delivered by authors, we shall not disparage our reader to repeat. Only the last and lasting part in their urns, collected bones and ashes, we cannot wholly omit, or decline that subject which occasion lately presented in some discovered among us.

In a field of old Walsingham, not many months past, were digged up between forty and fifty urns deposited in a dry and sandy soil not a yard deep, nor far from one another; not all strictly of one figure, but most answering these described; some containing two pounds of bones, distinguishable in skulls, ribs, jaws, thigh-bones, and teeth, with fresh impressions of their combustion, besides the extraneous substances, like pieces of small boxes, or combs handsomely wrought, handles of small brass instruments, brazen nippers, and in one some kind of opal.

Near the same plot of ground, for about six yards compass, were digged up coals and incinerated substances, which begat conjecture that this was the *ustrina* or place of burning their bodies, or some sacrificing place unto the *manes*,[1] which was properly below the surface of the ground, as the *arae*[2] and altars unto the gods and heroes above it.

That these were the urns of Romans, from the common custom and place where they were found, is no obscure conjecture; not far

---

38] refrain   39] David's son, whose name he cried out three times in mourning at the news of his death   40] merely artificial sets of rules   41] base their customs on the behaviour of animals   42] funeral rites

1] the spirits of the dead   2] altars dedicated to heroes or demi-gods

from a Roman garrison, and but five miles from Brancaster, set down by ancient record under the name of Brannodunum; and where the adjoining town, containing seven parishes, in no very different sound (but Saxon termination)[3] still retains the name of Burnham, which, being an early station, it is not improbable the neighbour parts were filled with habitations either of Romans themselves or Britons Romanised which observed the Roman customs.

Nor is it improbable that the Romans early possessed this country;[4] for though we meet not with such strict particulars of these parts before the new institution[5] of Constantine and military charge of the Count of the Saxon shore, and that about the Saxon invasions, the Dalmatian horsemen were in the garrison of Brancaster, yet in the time of Claudius, Vespasian, and Severus we find no less than three legions dispersed through the province of Britain. And as high as the reign of Claudius a great overthrow was given unto the Iceni[6] by the Roman lieutenant Ostorius. Not long after the country was so molested that in the hope of a better state Prasutagus bequeathed his kingdom unto Nero and his daughters; and Boadicea, his queen, fought the last decisive battle with Paulinus. After which time, and conquest of Agricola the lieutenant of Vespasian, probable it is they wholly possessed this country, ordering it into garrisons or habitations best suitable with their securities; and so some Roman habitations, not improbable in these parts, as high as the time of Vespasian, where the Saxons after seated, in whose thin-filled maps we yet find the name of Walsingham. Now if the Iceni were but Gammadims, Anconians,[7] or men that lived in an angle wedge or elbow of Britain, according to the original etymology, this country will challenge the emphatical appellation[8] as most properly making the elbow or 'iken' of Icenia.

That Britain was notably populous is undeniable, from that expression of Caesar.[9] That the Romans themselves were early in no small numbers, seventy thousand with their associates slain by Boadicea affords a sure account. And though many Roman habitations are now unknown, yet some by old works,[10] rampiers,[11] coins, and urns do testify their possessions. Some urns have been found at Caister, some also about Southcreek, and not many years past, no less than ten in a

3] the final syllable; Browne's etymology for Burnham is incorrect   4] region
5] legitimization of Christianity in the Roman empire in the fourth century.
6] the ancient people of East Anglia   7] the Gammadims were the people of Anconia (from the Greek for 'bend in the elbow')   8] i.e. the conventional 'Anglia'   9] noted in *Gallic Wars*   10] earthworks   11] bulwarks or buttresses

field at Buxton,[12] not near any recorded garrison. Nor is it strange to find Roman coins of copper and silver among us, of Vespasian, Trajan, Adrian, Commodus, Antoninus, Severus, etc. But the greater number of Diocletian, Constantine, Constans, Valens, with many of Victorinus, Posthumus, Tetricus, and the thirty tyrants in the reign of Gallienus; and some as high as Adrianus have been found about Thetford, or Sitomagus, mentioned in the itinerary of Antoninus as the way from Venta or Caister unto London. But the most frequent discovery is made at the two Caisters by Norwich and Yarmouth, at Burghcastle, and Brancaster. Besides the Norman, Saxon, and Danish pieces of Cuthred, Canutus, William, Matilda, and others, some British coins of gold have been dispersedly found, and no small number of silver pieces near Norwich, with a rude head upon the obverse, and an ill-formed horse on the reverse, with inscriptions *Ic. Duro. T.* whether implying Iceni, Durotriges, Tascia, or Trinobantes,[13] we leave to higher conjecture. Vulgar chronology will have Norwich Castle as old as Julius Caesar; but his distance from these parts, and its Gothic[14] form of structure, abridgeth such antiquity.[15] The British coins afford conjecture of early habitation in these parts, though the city of Norwich arose from the ruins of Venta,[16] and though perhaps not without some habitation before, was enlarged, builded, and nominated by the Saxons. In what bulk or populosity it stood in the old East Angle monarchy, tradition and history are silent. Considerable it was in Danish eruptions, when Sueno burnt Thetford and Norwich, and Ulfketel the governor thereof was able to make some resistance, and after endeavoured to burn the Danish navy.[17]

How the Romans left so many coins in countries of their conquests seems hard of resolution except we consider how they buried them underground, when upon barbarous invasions they were fain[18] to desert their habitations in most part of their empire; and the strictness of their laws forbidding to transfer them to any other uses; wherein the Spartans were singular, who, to make their copper money useless, contempered it with vinegar. That the Britons left any, some wonder, since their money was iron, and iron rings before Caesar; and those of after stamp by permission,[19] and but small in bulk and bigness. That so

12] towns in Norfolk   13] Durotriges, the Celtic people of Dorset and parts of the West country; tascia, tribute penny; Trinobantes, the ancient people of Essex and south Suffolk   14] of the Dark Ages   15] denies so old a date   16] the earlier city which Norwich replaced   17] Sweyn of Denmark conquered England; Ulfkell Snilling led the East Anglian forces against Sweyn in 1004   18] compelled   19] regular coinage by permission of the Roman rulers

few of the Saxons remain, because overcome by succeeding conquerors upon the place, their coins by degrees passed into other stamps, and the marks of after ages.

Than the time of these urns deposited, or precise antiquity of these relics, nothing of more uncertainty; for since the lieutenant of Claudius seems to have made the first progress into these parts, since Boadicea was overthrown by the forces of Nero, and Agricola put a full end to these conquests, it is not probable the country was fully garrisoned or planted before; and therefore, however these urns might be of later date, not likely of higher antiquity.

And the succeeding emperors desisted not from their conquests in these and other parts, as testified by history and medal inscription yet extant. The province of Britain is so divided a distance from Rome, beholding the faces[20] of many imperial persons, and in large account no fewer than Caesar, Claudius, Britannicus, Vespasian, Titus, Adrian, Severus, Commodus, Geta, and Caracalla.

A great obscurity herein,[21] because no medal or emperor's coin is enclosed which might denote the date of their interments, observable in many urns, and found in those of Spittle Fields by London, which contained the coins of Claudius, Vespasian, Commodus, Antoninus, attended with lachrymatories,[22] lamps, bottles of liquor,[23] and other appurtenances of affectionate superstition, which in these rural interments were wanting.

Some uncertainty there is from the period or term of burning, or the cessation of that practice. Macrobius affirmeth it was disused in his days. But most agree, though without authentic record, that it ceased with the Antonini – most safely to be understood, after the reign of those emperors which assumed the name of Antoninus, extending unto Heliogabalus. Not strictly after Marcus, for about fifty years later we find the magnificent burning and consecration of Severus; and if we so fix this period or cessation, these urns will challenge[24] above thirteen hundred years.

But whether this practice was only then left by emperors and great persons, or generally about Rome and not in other provinces, we hold no authentic account. For after Tertullian, in the days of Minucius, it was obviously objected upon Christians that they condemned the practice of burning. And we find a passage in Sidonius which asserteth that practice in France unto a lower account,[25] and perhaps not fully

---

20] imprinted on the coins   21] in the dates of the Norfolk urns   22] ceremonial tear-bottles   23] liquid   24] be as much as   25] a later date

disused till Christianity fully established, which gave the final extinction to these sepulchral bonfires.

Whether they were the bones of men or women or children, no authentic decision from ancient custom in distinct places of burial, although not improbably conjectured that the double sepulture[26] or burying place of Abraham had in it such intention;[27] but from exility[28] of bones, thinness of skulls, smallness of teeth, ribs, and thighbones, not improbable that many thereof were persons of minor age, or women, confirmable also from things contained in them: in most were found substances resembling combs, plates like boxes, fastened with iron pins, and handsomely overwrought like the necks or bridges of musical instruments, long brass plates overwrought like the handles of neat implements, brazen nippers to pull away hair, and in one a kind of opal yet maintaining a bluish colour.

Now, that they accustomed to burn or bury with them things wherein they excelled, delighted, or which were dear unto them, either as farewells unto all pleasure, or vain apprehension that they might use them in the other world, is testified by all antiquity; observable from the gem or beryl ring upon the finger of Cynthia, the mistress of Propertius, when after her funeral pyre her ghost appeared unto him. And notably illustrated from the contents of that Roman urn preserved by Cardinal Farnese, wherein, besides great number of gems with heads of gods and goddesses, were found an ape of agate, a grasshopper, an elephant of amber, a crystal ball, three glasses, two spoons, and six nuts of crystal. And beyond the content of urns, in the monument of Childeric the First, and fourth king from Pharamond, casually discovered three years past at Tournai, restoring unto the world much gold richly adorning his sword, two hundred rubies, many hundred imperial coins, three hundred golden bees, the bones and horeshoe of his horse interred with him, according to the barbarous magnificence of those days in their sepulchral obsequies. Although if we steer by the conjecture of many, and Septuagint expression, some trace thereof may be found even with the ancient Hebrews, not only from the sepulchral treasure of David, but the circumcision knives which Joshua also buried.

Some men considering the contents of these urns – lasting pieces and toys included in them – and the custom of burning with many other nations, might somewhat doubt whether all urns found among

26] a burying-place rather than a specific structure or tomb   27] designed to be the sepulchre of more than one person   28] thinness

us were properly Roman relics, or some not belonging unto our British, Saxon, and Danish forefathers.

In the form of burial among the ancient Britons, the large discourses of Caesar, Tacitus, and Strabo are silent; for the discovery whereof, with other particulars, we much deplore the loss of that letter which Cicero expected or received from his brother Quintus as a resolution of British customs; or the account which might have been made by Scribonius Largus, the physician accompanying the Emperor Claudius, who might have also discovered that frugal bit[29] of the old Britons, which in the bigness of a bean could satisfy their thirst and hunger.

But that the Druids and ruling priests used to burn and bury is expressed by Pomponius; that Bellinus the brother of Brennus and king of Britons was burnt is acknowledged by Polydorus. That they held that practice in Gallia Caesar expressly delivereth. Whether the Britons (probably descended from them, of like religion, language and manners) did not sometimes make use of burning, or whether at least such as were after civilised unto the Roman life and manners conformed not unto this practice, we have not historical assertion or denial. But since from the account of Tacitus the Romans early wrought so much civility upon the British stock that they brought them to build temples, to wear the gown, and study the Roman laws and language, that they conformed also unto their religious rites and customs in burials seems no improbable conjecture.

That burning the dead was used in Sarmatia is affirmed by Gaguinus; that the Sueons and Gothlanders[30] used to burn their princes and great persons is delivered by Saxo and Olaus; that this was the old German practice is also asserted by Tacitus. And although we are bare in historical particulars of such obsequies in this island, or that the Saxons, Jutes, and Angles burnt their dead, yet came they from parts where 'twas of ancient practice, the Germans using it, from whom they were descended. And even in Jutland and Sleswick in Anglis Cymbrica, urns with bones were found not many years before us.

But the Danish and northern nations have raised an era or point of compute from their custom of burning their dead,[31] some deriving it from Unguinus, some from Frotho the Great, who ordained by law that princes and chief commanders should be committed unto the fire,

29] a kind of expedition food made by the Britons, of which a bean-sized morsel was sufficient for a long period   30] Swedes and Goths   31] named an age after the practice of burning ('Roisold, Brendetiide, Ildtyde')

though the common sort had the common grave interment. So Starkatterus, that old hero, was burnt, and Ringo royally burnt the body of Harald the king slain by him.

What time this custom generally expired in that nation we discern no assured period; whether it ceased before Christianity, or upon their conversion by Ansgarius the Gaul in the time of Ludovicus Pius the son of Charles the Great, according to good computes; or whether it might not be used by some persons while for a hundred and eighty years paganism and Christianity were promiscuously embraced among them, there is no assured conclusion. About which times the Danes were busy in England, and particularly infested this country, where many castles and strongholds were built by them, or against them, and great number of names and families still derived from them. But since this custom was probably disused before their invasion or conquest, and the Romans confessedly practiced the same since their possession of this island, the most assured account will fall upon the Romans, or Britons Romanized.

However, certain it is that urns conceived of no Roman original are often digged up both in Norway, and Denmark, handsomely described and graphically represented by the learned physician Wormius; and in some parts of Denmark in no ordinary number, as stands delivered by authors exactly describing those countries. And they contained not only bones but many other substances in them, as knives, pieces of iron, brass and wood, and one of Norway a brass gilded Jew's-harp.

Nor were they confused or careless in disposing the noblest sort, while they placed large stones in circle about the urns, or bodies which they interred, somewhat answerable unto the monument of Rollrich stones[32] in England, or sepulchral monuments probably erected by Rollo, who after conquered Normandy, where[33] 'tis not improbable somewhat might be discovered. Meanwhile, to what nation or person belonged that large urn found at Ashbury containing mighty bones and a buckler, what[34] those large urns found at Little Massingham, or why the Anglesea urns are placed with their mouths downward, remains yet undiscovered.

32] the Rollright Stones, a stone circle in Oxfordshire   33] at Rollright
34] to what nation or person

¶ *Urn-Burial* Chapter III

Plastered and whited sepulchres were anciently affected in cadaverous
and corruptive burials; and the rigid Jews were wont to garnish the
sepulchres of the righteous; Ulysses in *Hecuba*[1] cared not how meanly
he lived, so he might find a noble tomb after death. Great persons
affected great monuments, and the fair and larger urns contained no
vulgar ashes, which makes that disparity[2] in those which time
discovereth among us. The present urns were not of one capacity, the
largest containing above a gallon, some not much above half that
measure; nor all of one figure, wherein there is no strict conformity in
the same or different countries, observable from those represented by
Casalius, Bosio, and others, though all found in Italy; while many have
handles, ears, and long necks, but most imitate a circular figure in a
spherical and round composure – whether from any mystery, best
duration, or capacity, were but a conjecture. But the common form
with necks was a proper figure,[3] making our last bed like our first, nor
much unlike the urns of our nativity, while we lay in the nether part of
the earth,[4] and inward vault of our microcosm. Many urns are red;
these but of a black colour, somewhat smooth, and dully sounding,
which begat some doubt whether they were burnt,[5] or only baked in
oven or sun, according to the ancient way in many bricks, tiles, pots,
and testaceous works, and as the word *testa*[6] is properly to be taken,
when occurring without addition; and chiefly intended by Pliny when
he commendeth bricks and tiles of two years old, and to make them in
the spring. Nor only these concealed pieces, but the open magnificence of antiquity, ran much in the artifice[7] of clay. Hereof the house
of Mausolus was built, thus old Jupiter stood in the Capitol, and the
statue of Hercules made in the reign of Tarquinius Priscus was extant
in Pliny's days. And such as declined burning or funeral urns, affected
coffins of clay, according to the mode of Pythagoras and way preferred
by Varro. But the spirit of great ones was above these circumscrip-
tions,[8] affecting copper, silver, gold, and porphyry urns, wherein
Severus lay, after a serious view and sentence on that which should
contain him.[9] Some of these urns were thought to have been silvered

1] a play by Euripides   2] in degrees of sumptuousness   3] bodily shape
4] 'But those that seek my soul, to destroy it, shall go into the lower part of the
earth' (Psalm 63:9)   5] fired in a kiln   6]* testaceous means 'having a shell',
but Browne invents an homophonic adjective from *testa* ('potsherd') to refer to
earthenware   7] craftsmanship, working   8] limitation to clay   9] Severus
said of his own urn, 'Thou shalt hold a man that the world could not hold' (Dio
Cassius 77.15)

over, from sparklings in several pots, with small tinsel parcels, uncertain whether from the earth, or the first mixture in them.

Among these urns we could obtain no good account of their coverings; only one seemed arched over with some kind of brickwork. Of those found at Buxton some were covered with flints, some in other parts with tiles, those at Yarmouth Caister[10] were closed with Roman bricks; and some have proper earthen covers adapted and fitted to them. But in the Homerical urn of Patroclus, whatever was the solid tegument,[11] we find the immediate covering to be a purple piece of silk; and such as had no covers might have the earth closely pressed into them, after which disposure were probably some of these, wherein we found the bones and ashes half mortared unto the sand and sides of the urn; and some long roots of quitch, or dog's grass, wreathed about the bones.

No lamps, included liquors, lachrymatories, or tear-bottles attended these rural urns, either as sacred unto the *manes,* or passionate expressions of their surviving friends, while with rich flames and hired tears they solemnised their obsequies, and in the most lamented monuments made one part of their inscriptions.[12] Some find sepulchral vessels containing liquors, which time hath incrassated[13] into jellies, for beside these lachrymatories, notable lamps with vessels of oils and aromatical liquors attended noble ossuaries;[14] and some yet retaining a vinosity[15] and spirit in them, which if any have tasted they have far exceeded the palates of antiquity,[16] liquors not to be computed by years of annual magistrates, but by great conjunctions and the fatal periods of kingdoms.[17] The draughts of consulary date[18] were but crude unto these, and Opimian[19] wine but in the must[20] to them.

In sundry graves and sepulchres we meet with rings, coins, and chalices. Ancient frugality was so severe that they allowed no gold to attend the corpse, but only that which served to fasten their teeth. Whether the opaline stone in this urn were burnt upon the finger of the dead, or cast into the fire by some affectionate friend, it will consist with either custom. But other incinerable substances were found so fresh that they could feel no singe from fire. These upon view were

10] as the name suggests, originally a Roman settlement   11] covering or coating   12] i.e. tears   13] condensed   14 receptacles for bones   15] wine-like quality   16] they will have tasted something no ancient could ever have tasted   17] 'about five hundred years'   18] vintages reckoned by the numeration of a consul's years in office   19] wine made in the consulate of Opimian, and especially of the year 121 BC   20] wine in an early and incomplete state of fermentation

judged to be wood, but sinking in water and tried by fire, we found them to be bone or ivory. In their hardness and yellow colour they most resembled box, which in old expressions found the epithet of eternal,[21] and perhaps in such conservatories might have passed uncorrupted.

That bay leaves were found green in the tomb of St Humbert after an hundred and fifty years was looked upon as miraculous. Remarkable it was unto old spectators that the cypress of the Temple of Diana lasted so many hundred years. The wood of the ark and olive rod of Aaron were older at the captivity.[22] But the cypress of the ark of Noah was the greatest vegetable antiquity, if Josephus were not deceived by some fragments of it in his days (to omit the moor-logs[23] and fir trees found underground in many parts of England, the undated ruins of winds, floods or earthquakes, and which in Flanders still show from what quarter they fell, as generally lying in a northeast position).

But though we found not these pieces to be wood, according to first apprehension, yet we missed not altogether of some woody substance, for the bones were not so clearly picked, but some coals were found amongst them – a way to make wood perpetual, and a fit associate for metal, whereon was laid the foundation of the great Ephesian temple,[24] and which were made the lasting tests of old boundaries and landmarks. Whilst we look on these, we admire not observations of coals found fresh after four hundred years. In a long deserted habitation, even eggshells have been found fresh, not tending to corruption.

In the monument of King Childeric the iron relics were found all rusty and crumbling into pieces. But our little iron pins which fastened the ivory works[25] held well together and lost not their magnetical quality, though wanting a tenacious moisture for the firmer union of parts. Although it be hardly[26] drawn into fusion, yet that metal soon submitteth unto rust and dissolution. In the brazen pieces, we admired not the duration but the freedom from rust and ill savour[27] upon the hardest attrition;[28] but now exposed unto the piercing atoms of air, in the space of a few months they begin to spot and betray their green entrails. We conceive not these urns to have descended thus naked as they appear or to have entered their graves without the old habit of flowers. The urn of Philopoemen was so laden with flowers

21] were commonly called 'eternal' (box is scientifically known as *Buxus sempervirens*)   22] the captivity of the Israelites   23] remains of trees found in bogs   24] the temple of Diana or Apollo at Ephesus   25] relics of ivory included in the urn burial   26] [drawn into] hard [fusion]   27] decay or tarnish   28] severest rubbing away, wearing down

and ribbons that it afforded no sight of itself. The rigid Lycurgus allowed olive and myrtle. The Athenians might fairly except against the practice of Democritus to be buried up in honey, as fearing to embezzle a great commodity of their country and the best of that kind in Europe. But Plato seems too frugally politic, who allowed no larger monument than would contain four heroic[29] verses, and designed the most barren ground for sepulture; though we cannot commend the goodness of that sepulchral ground[30] which was set at no higher rate than the mean salary of Judas. Though the earth had confounded the ashes of these ossuaries, yet the bones were so smartly burnt that some thin plates of brass were found half melted among them, whereby we apprehend they were not of the meanest carcasses, perfunctorily fired as sometimes in military, and commonly in pestilence, burnings; or after the manner of abject corpses huddled forth and carelessly burnt without the Esquiline Port at Rome, which was an affront[31] contrived upon Tiberius while they but half burnt his body, and in the amphitheatre, according to the custom in notable malefactors; whereas Nero seemed not so much to fear his death as that his head should be cut off and his body not burnt entire.

Some finding many fragments of skulls in these urns, suspected a mixture of bones. In none we searched was there cause of such conjecture, though sometimes they declined not that practice: the ashes of Domitian were mingled with those of Julia;[32] of Achilles with those of Patroclus. All urns contained not single ashes: without confused burnings they affectionately compounded their bones, passionately endeavouring to continue their living unions. And when distance of death denied such conjunctions, unsatisfied affections conceived some satisfaction to be neighbours in the grave, to lie urn by urn and touch but in their names. And many were so curious[33] to continue their living relations that they contrived large and family urns wherein the ashes of their nearest friends and kindred might successively be received, at least some parcels thereof, while their collateral[34] memorials lay in minor vessels about them.

Antiquity held too light thoughts from objects of mortality, while some drew provocatives of mirth from anatomies,[35] and jugglers

29] hexameter   30] the potter's field, bought with Judas' thirty pieces of silver, in which were buried strangers   31] corpses of the poor, criminals, and the disgraced were thrown from the Esquiline Port to be burnt or eaten by dogs
32] Domitian was responsible for the death of his niece Julia, and the nurse who had raised them both cremated him and placed his ashes with hers   33] eager
34] of relations   35] skeletons, dessicated bodies, or dissected bodies

showed tricks with skeletons; when fiddlers made not so pleasant mirth as fencers, and men could sit with quiet stomachs while hanging was played before them.[36] Old considerations made few mementoes by skulls and bones upon their monuments. In the old Egyptian obelisks and hieroglyphical figures it is not easy to meet with bones. The sepulchral lamps speak nothing less than sepulture,[37] and in their literal draughts prove often obscene and antic pieces. Where we find D.M.[38] it is obvious to meet with sacrificing *pateras*[39] and vessels of libation upon old sepulchral monuments. In the Jewish hypogaeum[40] and subterranean cell at Rome was little observable beside the variety of lamps, and frequent draughts of the holy candlestick.[41] In authentic draughts of Antony and Jerome[42] we meet with thigh-bones and death's heads; but the cemeterial cells of ancient Christians and martyrs were filled with draughts of stories, not declining the flourishes of cypress, palms, and olive, and the mystical figures of peacocks, doves and cocks,[43] but iterately[44] affecting the portraits of Enoch, Lazarus, Jonas, and the vision of Ezekiel[45] as hopeful draughts and hinting imagery of the Resurrection, which is the life of the grave, and sweetens our habitations in the land of moles and pismires.

Gentile inscriptions precisely delivered the extent of men's lives, seldom the manner of their deaths, which history itself so often leaves obscure in the records of memorable persons. There is scarce any philosopher but dies twice or thrice in Laertius, nor almost any life without two or three deaths in Plutarch, which makes the tragical ends of noble persons more favourably resented[46] by compassionate readers, who find some relief in the election[47] of such differences.

The certainty of death is attended with uncertainties in time, manner, places. The variety of monuments hath often obscured true graves, and cenotaphs confounded sepulchres;[48] for beside their real tombs, many have founded honorary and empty sepulchres. The vari-

36] 'A barbarous pastime at feasts, when men stood upon a rolling globe, with their necks in a rope fastened to a beam, and a knife in their hands, ready to cut it when the stone was rolled away, wherein if they failed they lost their lives to the laughter of their spectators.'   37] grave-lamps indicate burial in a vault   38] *Diis manibus* ('To the gods of the underworld')   39] offertorial dishes in sacrifices   40] burial vault   41] the menorah, or seven-fold candlestick   42] St Antony lived in a tomb as a hermit; St Jerome visited the Roman catacombs   43] various plants and birds of hieroglyphical significance to early Christians   44] repeatedly   45] the first three ascended to heaven; in Ezekiel's vision a valley full of bones reformed itself into separate fleshed-out bodies which God told him was a sign of resurrection (Ezekiel 37:1-12)   46] felt   47] choice   48] memorial monuments have been confused with actual graves

ety of Homer's monuments made him of various countries. Euripides had his tomb in Attica, but his sepulture in Macedonia, and Severus found his real sepulchre in Rome, but his empty grave in Gallia.

He that lay in a golden urn[49] eminently above the earth was not likely to find the quiet of these bones. Many of these urns were broke by a vulgar discoverer in hope of enclosed treasure. The ashes of Marcellus[50] were lost above ground upon the like account. Where profit hath prompted, no age hath wanted such miners; for which the most barbarous expilators[51] found the most civil rhetoric: gold once out of the earth is no more due unto it; what was unreasonably committed to the ground is reasonably resumed from it; let monuments and rich fabrics, not riches, adorn men's ashes; the commerce of the living is not to be transferred unto the dead; it is no injustice to take that which none complains to lose, and no man is wronged where no man is possessor.

What virtue yet sleeps in this *terra damnata*[52] and aged cinders were petty magic to experiment: these crumbling relics and long-fired particles superannuate such expectations. Bones, hairs, nails, and teeth of the dead, were the treasures of old sorcerers. In vain we revive such practices: present superstition too visibly perpetuates the folly of our forefathers, wherein unto old observation this island was so complete that it might have instructed Persia.[53]

Plato's historian of the other world[54] lies twelve days incorrupted while his soul was viewing the large stations of the dead. How to keep the corpse seven days from corruption by annointing and washing, without exentration,[55] were an hazardable piece of art[56] in our choicest practice. How they made distinct separation of bones and ashes from fiery admixture hath found no historical solution, though they seemed to make a distinct collection,[57] and overlooked not Pyrrhus his toe.[58] Some provision they might make by fictile vessels,[59] coverings, tiles, or flat stones upon and about the body (and in the same field, not far from these urns, many stones were found underground), as also by careful separation of extraneous matter, composing and raking up the burnt

49] Trajan   50] who fell in battle against Hannibal in southern Italy. Hannibal had his ashes sent to Rome in a sumptuous urn, but when it was seized and despoiled along the way, Hannibal left the ashes where they lay, regarding it as a divinely ordained fate   51] plunderers   52] 'damned earth', an alchemical term for the residue after burning   53] Pliny says that England might have been an example in its superstitious ceremonies to the country most notorious for it, and from whom the magic was derived (Pliny 30.4)   54] Er in the *Republic*
55] evisceration   56] difficult feat to perform   57] gathering up
58] 'which could not be burnt'   59] pottery

bones with forks, observable in that notable lamp of Galvanus.[60] Marlianus, who had the sight of the *vas ustrinum*[61] or vessel wherein they burnt the dead, found in the Esquiline field at Rome, might have afforded clearer solution. But their insatisfaction herein begat that remarkable invention in the funeral pyres of some princes, by incombustible sheets made with a texture of asbestos (incremable[62] flax, or salamander's wool), which preserved their bones and ashes incommixed.[63]

How the bulk of a man should sink into so few pounds of bones and ashes may seem strange unto any who considers not its constitution, and how slender a mass will remain upon an open and urging fire of the carnal composition. Even bones themselves reduced into ashes do abate a notable proportion, and consisting much of a volatile salt, when that is fired out, make a light kind of cinders, although their bulk be disproportionable to their weight, when the heavy principle of salt is fired out, and the earth almost only remaineth; observable in sallow,[64] which makes more ashes than oak, and discovers the common fraud of selling ashes by measure and not by ponderation.[65]

Some bones make best skeletons,[66] some bodies quick and speediest ashes: who would expect a quick flame from hydropical[67] Heraclitus? The poisoned soldier, when his belly brake, put out two pyres in Plutarch.[68] But in the plague of Athens, one private pyre served two or three intruders;[69] and the Saracens burnt in large heaps by the King of Castile, showed how little fuel sufficeth. Though the funeral pyre of Patroclus took up an hundred foot, a piece of an old boat burnt Pompey,[70] and if the burthen of Isaac[71] were sufficient for an holocaust,[72] a man may carry his own pyre.

From animals are drawn good burning lights and good medicines against burning; though the seminal humour[73] seems of a contrary nature to fire, yet the body completed proves a combustible lump, wherein fire finds flame even from bones, and some fuel almost from

60] a lamp decorated with pictures of ancient funeral rites   61] a pyre or oven
62] incombustible   63] unmixed   64] willow   65] weight   66] especially those of old people or small thin young people, according to Brown
67] dropsical, the accumulation of water in the connective tissue   68] foul play was suspected when one of Tiberius' friends died suddenly and his body exploded with the pressure of purulent matter inside, dousing his funeral pyre and making it impossible to be relit   69] foreigners   70] who was assassinated and thrown onto the seashore, where one of his centurions burned his body in the remains of an old fishing boat   71] Abraham had Isaac carry the wood which was to be used in his own sacrifice (Genesis 22:6)   72] complete destruction by fire
73] spermaceti oil, which was thought to be the semen of whales

all parts, though the metropolis of humidity[74] seems least disposed
unto it, which might render the skulls of these urns less burned than
other bones. But all flies or sinks before fire almost in all bodies; when
the common ligament is dissolved, the attenuable parts ascend, the
rest subside in coal, calx,[75] or ashes.

To burn the bones of the King of Edom for lime[76] seems no irra-
tional ferity;[77] but to drink of the ashes of dead relations, a passionate
prodigality.[78] He that hath the ashes of his friend, hath an everlasting
treasure; where fire taketh leave, corruption slowly enters; in bones
well burnt, fire makes a wall against itself,[79] experimented in copels[80]
and tests of metals which consist of such ingredients. What the sun
compoundeth, fire analyseth, not transmuteth.[81] That devouring
agent leaves almost always a morsel for the earth, whereof all things are
but a colony, and which, if time permits, the mother element[82] will
have in their primitive mass again.

He that looks for urns and old sepulchral relics must not seek them
in the ruins of temples, where no religion anciently placed them.
These were found in a field, according to ancient custom in noble or
private burial – the old practice of the Canaanites, the family of
Abraham, and the burying place of Joshua, in the borders of his possessions – and also agreeable unto Roman practice to bury by high-
ways, whereby their monuments were under eye, memorials of themselves, and mementoes of mortality unto living passengers, whom the
epitaphs of great ones were fain to beg to stay and look upon them, a
language though sometimes used, not so proper in church inscriptions. The sensible[83] rhetoric of the dead, to exemplarity of[84] good life,
first admitted the bones of pious men and martyrs within church walls,
which in succeeding ages crept into promiscuous practice; while
Constantine was peculiarly favoured to be admitted unto the church
porch, and the first thus buried in England was in the days of Cuthred.

Christians dispute how their bodies should lie in the grave. In urnal
interment they clearly escaped this controversy. Though we decline
the religious consideration,[85] yet in cemeterial and narrower burying
places, to avoid confusion and cross position, a certain posture were to

---

74] the brain   75] powdered lime residue produced by burning   76] a divine
retribution (Amos 2:1)   77] barbarity   78] 'As Artemisia of her husband
Mausolus'   79] certain substances by being fired are made incombustible
80] dishes used in the assaying of metals   81] to mix elements, separate them
out from a compound, and change them into another element (alchemical)
82] earth   83] perceptible to the senses   84] exemplify   85] doctrinal
attitudes

be admitted, which even pagan civility observed. The Persians lay north and south, the Megarians[86] and Phoenicians placed their heads to the east, the Athenians, some think, toward the west, which Christians still retain. And Beda will have it to be the posture of our Saviour. That he was crucified with his face towards the west, we will not contend with tradition and probable account; but we applaud not the hand of the painter in exalting his cross so high above those on either side,[87] since hereof we find no authentic account in history, and even the crosses found by Helena pretend no such distinction from longitude or dimension.

To be gnawed[88] out of our graves, to have our skulls made drinking bowls, and our bones turned into pipes to delight and sport our enemies, are tragical abominations escaped in burning burials.

Urnal interments and burnt relics lie not in fear of worms, or to be an heritage[89] for serpents. In carnal sepulture, corruptions seem peculiar unto parts, and some speak of snakes out of the spinal marrow. But while we suppose common worms in graves, 'tis not easy to find any there; few in churchyards above a foot deep, fewer or none in churches, though in fresh decayed bodies. Teeth, bones, and hair give the most lasting defiance to corruption. In an hydropical body ten years buried in a churchyard, we met with a fat concretion where the nitre of the earth and the salt and lixivious[90] liquor of the body had coagulated large lumps of fat into the consistence of the hardest castle-soap, whereof part remaineth with us.[91] After a battle with the Persians the Roman corpses decayed a few days, while the Persian bodies remained dry and uncorrupted. Bodies in the same ground do not uniformly dissolve, nor bones equally moulder; whereof in the opprobrious disease[92] we expect no long duration. The body of the Marquis of Dorset seemed sound and handsomely cereclothed,[93] that after seventy-eight years was found uncorrupted. Common tombs preserve not beyond powder. A firmer consistence and compage[94] of parts might be expected from arefaction,[95] deep burial, or charcoal. The greatest antiquities of mortal bodies may remain in petrified bones whereof, though we take not in the pillar of Lot's wife, or metamorphosis of Ortelius,[96] some may be older than pyramids in the petrified relics of

86] a people of Corinth   87] the two thieves crucified at the same time as Christ   88] this word appears as 'knav'd' in the original, and may well be correct ('to knave', to steal)   89] portion   90] alkaline   91] adipocere or grave wax   92 probably syphilis   93] wrapped in a winding-sheet of waxed fabric   94] solid and compact structure   95] process of drying   96] a map of Russia in Ortelius' *Theatrum orbum Terrarum* (1574) 'Wherein great numbers of men, oxen, and sheep were petrified.'

the general inundation.[97] When Alexander opened the tomb of Cyrus, the remaining bones discovered his proportion, whereof urnal fragments afford but a bad conjecture and have this disadvantage of grave interments, that they leave us ignorant of most personal discoveries. For since bones afford not only rectitude and stability but figure unto the body, it is no impossible physiognomy[98] to conjecture at fleshy appendencies, and after what shape the muscles and carnous parts might hang in their full consistences. A full spread cariola[99] shows a well-shaped horse behind; handsome-formed skulls give some analogy of fleshy resemblance. A critical view of bones makes a good distinction of sexes. Even colour is not beyond conjecture, since it is hard to be deceived in the distinction of negroes' skulls. Dante's characters are to be found in skulls as well as faces.[100] Hercules is not only known by his foot. Other parts make out their comproportions[101] and inferences upon whole or parts. And since the dimensions of the head measure the whole body,[102] and the figure thereof gives conjecture of the principal faculties, physiognomy outlives ourselves, and ends not in our graves.

Severe contemplators observing these lasting relics may think them good monuments of persons past, little advantage to future beings. And considering that power which subdueth all things unto itself, that can resume the scattered atoms or identify out of anything,[103] conceive it superfluous to expect a resurrection out of relics. But, the soul subsisting, other matter (clothed with due accidents) may salve the individuality.[104] Yet the saints, we observe, arose from graves and monuments about the Holy City. Some think the ancient Patriarchs so earnestly desired to lay their bones in Canaan, as hoping to make a part of that resurrection, and though thirty miles from Mount Calvary, at least to lie in that region which should produce the first fruits of the dead. And if according to learned conjecture the bodies of men shall rise where their greatest relics remain, many are not like to err in the topography of their resurrection, though their bones or bodies be after translated by angels into the field of Ezekiel's vision, or as some will order it, into the valley of judgement, or Jehosaphat.

97] the flood   98] facial features; the art of conjecturing abstract characteristics of personality from physical features   99] haunch bones   100] Dante sees the figure 'omo' (homo) made by the arch of the brow ('m') between the two eyes ('o', 'o')   101]* common/joint proportion   102] from the size of the head the proportions of the body can be worked out   103] determine a single thing, or make one, out of many parts   104] the soul's character will be recognizable, whatever the outer features of the body it inhabits

¶ *Urn-Burial* Chapter IV

Christians have handsomely glossed the deformity of death by careful consideration of the body and civil rites which take off brutal terminations. And though they conceived all reparable by a resurrection, cast not off all care of interment. For since the ashes of sacrifices burnt upon the altar of God were carefully carried out by the priests and deposed in a clean field, since they acknowledged their bodies to be the lodging of Christ, and temples of the Holy Ghost, they devolved not all upon the sufficiency of soul existence;[1] and therefore with long services and full solemnities concluded their last exequies, wherein to all distinctions the Greek devotion seems most pathetically ceremonious.[2]

Christian invention hath chiefly driven at rites which speak hopes of another life and hints of a resurrection. And if the ancient Gentiles held not the immortality of their better part and some subsistence after death, in several rites, customs, actions, and expressions, they contradicted their own opinions, wherein Democritus went high, even to the thought of a resurrection, as scoffingly recorded by Pliny.[3] What can be more express than the expression of Phocyllides?[4] Or who would expect from Lucretius a sentence of Ecclesiastes?[5] Before Plato could speak, the soul had wings in Homer which fell not, but flew out of the body into the mansions of the dead; who[6] also observed that handsome distinction of *demas* and *soma*,[7] for the body conjoined to the soul and body separated from it. Lucian spoke much truth in jest when he said that part of Hercules which proceeded from Alcmena perished, that from Jupiter remained immortal.[8] Thus Socrates was content that his friends should bury his body, so they would not think they buried Socrates, and regarding only his immortal part, was indifferent to be burnt or buried. From such considerations Diogenes might contemn sepulture, and being satisfied that the soul could not perish, grow careless of corporal interment. The Stoics, who thought the souls of wise men had their habitation about the moon, might make slight account of subterraneous deposition; whereas the Pythagoreans and

1] they did not neglect the body in favour of the soul   2] the Greek Orthodox ceremony tends toward pathos   3] 'A similar vanity is the resurrection promised by Democritus, who has not himself come back to life. What evil, how mad it is, to think to return to life after death?'   4] 'We hope that perhaps the remains of the departed may return from the earth into the light'   5] 'That even comes back to the earth which was in the earth before'; this gnomic remark is reminiscent of the style of Ecclesiastes   6] Homer   7] in Greek, the living and the dead body   8] when Hercules' body was burned, he threw off his mortal part, and became immortal owing to his heritage from Zeus

the transcorporating philosophers,[9] who were to be often buried,[10] held great care of their interment. And the Platonics rejected not a due care of the grave, though they put their ashes to unreasonable expectations in their tedious term of return and long set revolution.[11]

Men have lost their reason in nothing so much as their religion, wherein stones and clouts make martyrs; and since the religion of one seems madness unto another, to afford an account or rationale of old rites requires no rigid reader. That they kindled the pyre aversely, or turning their face from it, was an handsome symbol of unwilling ministration; that they washed their bones with wine and milk, that the mother wrapped them in linen, and dried them in her bosom, the first fostering part, and place of their nourishment; that they opened their eyes towards heaven before they kindled the fire, as the place of their hopes or original, were no improper ceremonies. Their last valediction[12] thrice uttered by the attendants was also very solemn, and somewhat answered by Christians, who thought it too little if they threw not the earth thrice upon the interred body. That in strewing their tombs the Romans affected the rose, the Greeks amaranthus and myrtle; that the funeral pyre consisted of sweet fuel, cypress, fir, larix,[13] yew, and trees perpetually verdant, lay silent expressions of their surviving hopes; wherein Christians which deck their coffins with bays have found a more elegant emblem:[14] for that tree, seeming dead, will restore itself from the root, and its dry and exsuccous[15] leaves resume their verdure again, which, if we mistake not, we have also observed in furze.[16] Whether the planting of yew in churchyards hold not its original from ancient funeral rites, or as an emblem of resurrection from its perpetual verdure, may also admit conjecture.

They made use of music to excite or quiet the affections of their friends, according to different harmonies. But the secret and symbolical hint was the harmonical nature of the soul which, delivered from the body, went again to enjoy the primitive harmony of heaven,[17] from whence it first descended; which according to its progress traced by antiquity, came down by Cancer, and ascended by Capricornus.[18]

They burnt not children before their teeth appeared, as apprehend-

9] who believed in transmigration of the soul   10] since they believed in a kind of perpetual reincarnation, they would expect to live and die many times 11] they expected time to revolve endlessly in thousand year cycles, and their ashes therefore to be preserved   12] 'Farewell, farewell, farewell, we will follow you in the order which nature permits'   13] larch   14] a more exact visual equivalent of their hopes (in the ability of bay to rejuvenate itself from the root) 15] sapless   16] gorse   17] the music of the spheres   18] the two tropics were deemed the exit and entrance of heaven

ing their bodies too tender a morsel for fire, and that their gristly bones would scarce leave separable relics after the pyral combustion. That they kindled not fire in their houses for some days after was a strict memorial of the late afflicting fire. And mourning without hope, they had an happy fraud against excessive lamentation, by a common opinion that deep sorrows disturbed their ghosts.

That they buried their dead on their backs, or in a supine position, seems agreeable unto profound sleep and common posture of dying, contrary to the most natural way of birth, nor like our pendulous posture in the doubtful state of the womb. Diogenes was singular, who preferred a prone situation in the grave; and some Christians like neither, who decline the figure of rest and make choice of an erect posture.

That they carried them out of the world with their feet forward, not inconsonant unto reason, as contrary unto the native posture of man and his production first unto it, and also agreeable unto their opinions, while they bid adieu unto the world, not to look again upon it; whereas Mahometans, who think to return to a delightful life again, are carried forth with their heads forward, and looking toward their houses.

They closed their eyes as parts which first die or first discover the sad effects of death. But their iterated clamations[19] to excitate their dying or dead friends or revoke them unto life again was a vanity of affection, as not presumably ignorant of the critical tests of death, by apposition of feathers, glasses, and reflection of figures,[20] which dead eyes represent not; which, however not strictly verifiable in fresh and warm cadavers, could hardly elude the test in corpses of four or five days.

That they sucked in the last breath of their expiring friends was surely a practice of no medical institution, but a loose opinion that the soul passed out that way, and a fondness of affection from Pythagorical foundation, that the spirit of one body passed into another, which they wished might be their own.

That they poured oil upon the pyre was a tolerable practice while the intention rested in facilitating the accension;[21] but to place good omens in the quick and speedy burning, to sacrifice unto the winds for a dispatch in this office was a low form of superstition.

The archmime or jester attending the funeral train and imitating the speeches, gesture, and manners of the deceased was too light for such solemnities, contradicting their funeral orations and doleful rites of the grave.

19] cries   20] application of feathers and mirrors to the mouth to test for breathing, and of looking for a reflection of objects in the eyes   21] kindling

That they buried a piece of money with them as a fee of the Elysian ferryman[22] was a practice full of folly. But the ancient custom of placing coins in considerable urns, and the present practice of burying medals in the noble foundations[23] of Europe are laudable ways of historical discoveries in actions, persons, chronologies, and posterity will applaud them.

We examine not the old laws of sepulture exempting certain persons from burial or burning. But hereby we apprehend that these were not the bones of persons planet-struck or burnt with fire from heaven,[24] no relics of traitors to their country, self-killers, or sacrilegious malefactors – persons in old apprehension unworthy of the earth, condemned unto the Tartarus[25] of hell and bottomless pit of Pluto, from whence there was no redemption.

Nor were only many customs questionable in order to their obsequies, but also sundry practices, fictions, and conceptions, discordant or obscure, of their state and future beings: whether unto eight or ten bodies of men to add one of a woman as being more inflammable and unctuously constituted[26] for the better pyral combustion were any rational practice, or whether the complaint of Periander's wife be tolerable, that wanting her funeral burning she suffered intolerable cold in hell, according to the constitution of the infernal house of Pluto wherein cold makes a great part of their tortures, it cannot pass without some question.

Why the female ghosts appear unto Ulysses before the heroes and masculine spirits? Why the psyche or soul of Tiresias is of the masculine gender, who, being blind on earth, sees more than all the rest in hell? Why the funeral suppers consisted of eggs, beans, smallage,[27] and lettuce, since the dead are made to eat asphodels[28] about the Elysian meadows? Why, since there is no sacrifice acceptable, nor any propitiation for the covenant of the grave, men set up the deity of Morta and fruitlessly adore divinities without ears, it cannot escape some doubt.

The dead seem all alive in the humane[29] Hades of Homer, yet cannot well speak, prophesy, or know the living, except they drink blood wherein is the life of man. And therefore the souls of Penelope's paramours conducted by Mercury chirped like bats,[30] and those which followed Hercules made a noise but like a flock of birds.

22] Charon   23] new institutions such as colleges and libraries   24] killed by the influence of a heavenly body or struck down by lightning   25] the lowest region of the underworld   26] fatty   27] celery or parsley   28] a type of lily said to grow in the meadows of Elysium, the afterworld of the Blessed in early Greek mythology   29]* classical   30] in the *Odyssey* XXIV. 4-10

The departed spirits know things past and to come, yet are ignorant of things present. Agamemnon foretells what should happen unto Ulysses, yet ignorantly enquires what is become of his own son.[31] The ghosts are afraid of swords in Homer, yet, Sybilla tells Aeneas in Vergil,[32] the thin habit of spirits was beyond the force of weapons. The spirits put off their malice with their bodies, and Caesar and Pompey accord[33] in Latin hell, yet Ajax in Homer endures not a conference with Ulysses; and Deiphobus appears all mangled in Vergil's ghosts, yet we meet with perfect shadows among the wounded ghosts of Homer.

Since Charon in Lucian applauds his condition among the dead, whether it be handsomely said of Achilles, that living contemner of death, that he had rather be a ploughman's servant than emperor of the dead? How Hercules his soul is in hell, and yet in heaven,[34] and Julius[35] his soul in a star, yet seen by Aeneas in hell, except the ghosts were but images and shadows of the soul, received in higher mansions, according to the ancient division of body, soul, and image or simulacrum of them both. The particulars of future beings must needs be dark unto ancient theories, which Christian philosophy yet determines but in a cloud of opinions. A dialogue between two infants in the womb concerning the state of this world might handsomely illustrate our ignorance of the next, whereof methinks we yet discourse in Plato's den,[36] and are but embryon philosophers.

Pythagoras escapes in the fabulous hell of Dante among that swarm of philosophers, wherein, whilst we meet with Plato and Socrates, Cato is to be found in no lower place than purgatory. Among all the set, Epicurus is most considerable, whom men make honest without an Elysium, who contemned life without encouragement of immortality, and making nothing after death, yet made nothing of the king of terrors.

Were the happiness of the next world as closely apprehended as the felicities of this, it were a martyrdom to live; and unto such as consider none hereafter, it must be more than death to die, which makes us amazed at those audacities[37] that durst be nothing and return unto their chaos again. Certainly such spirits as could contemn death, when they expected no better being after, would have scorned to live had

31] the ghost of Agamemnon foretells that Penelope will not slaughter her husband Ulysses as Clytemnestra did Agamemnon　　32] the sybil in the *Aeneid*　　33] make peace　　34] *Odyssey* xi.717-31　　35] Caesar, deified (like many Roman rulers) after death　　36] the cave, in which the world is but the flickering of shadows on the wall, an indistinct version of its ideal form　　37] beliefs which deny any afterlife

they known any. And therefore we applaud not the judgement of Machiavel, that Christianity makes men cowards, or that with the confidence of but half dying, the despised virtues of patience and humility have abased the spirits of men, which pagan principles exalted, but rather regulated the wildness of audacities, in the attempts, grounds, and eternal sequels of death,[38] wherein men of the boldest spirits are often prodigiously temerarious.[39] Nor can we extenuate[40] the valour of ancient martyrs who contemned death in the uncomfortable scene of their lives, and in their decrepit martyrdoms did probably lose not many months of their days, or parted with life when it was scarce worth the living. For (beside that long time past holds no consideration unto a slender time to come) they had no small disadvantage from the constitution of old age, which naturally makes men fearful, complexionally superannuated[41] from the bold and courageous thoughts of youth and fervent years. But the contempt of death from corporal animosity promoteth not our felicity. They may sit in the orchestra and noblest seats of heaven who have held up shaking hands in the fire and humanly contended for glory.

Meanwhile Epicurus lies deep in Dante's hell, wherein we meet with tombs enclosing souls which denied their immortalities. But whether the virtuous heathen,[42] who lived better than he spake or, erring in the principles of himself, yet lived above philosophers of more specious maxims, lie so deep as he is placed, at least so low as not to rise against Christians who believing or knowing that truth have lastingly denied it in their practice and conversation, were a query too sad to insist on.

But all or most apprehensions rested in opinions of some future being, which, ignorantly or coldly believed, begat those perverted conceptions, ceremonies, sayings, which Christians pity or laugh at. Happy are they which live not in that disadvantage of time when men could say little for futurity[43] but from reason. Whereby the noblest minds fell often upon doubtful deaths and melancholy dissolutions: with these hopes Socrates warmed his doubtful spirits against that cold potion, and Cato before he durst give the fatal stroke spent part of the night in reading the immortality of Plato, thereby confirming his wavering hand unto the animosity of that attempt.

It is the heaviest stone that melancholy can throw at a man, to tell

38] various aspects of death and the afterlife   39] reckless, rash   40] discount   41] temperamentally outgrown   42] the good men (including Old Testament figures) who lived before Christ and therefore could not apparently be saved   43] in modern times when there is little left to expect except what the sorry example of the past permits him he is at the end of his nature, or that there is no further state to come unto which this seems progressional, and otherwise made in vain. Without this accomplishment the natural expectation and desire of such a state were but a fallacy in nature; unsatisfied considerators would quarrel the justice of their constitutions, and rest content that Adam had fallen lower, whereby by knowing no other original and deeper ignorance of themselves, they might have enjoyed the happiness of inferior creatures, who in tranquillity possess their constitutions as having not the apprehension to deplore their own natures. And being framed below the circumference of these hopes or cognition of better being, the wisdom of God hath necessitated their contentment. But the superior ingredient and obscured part of ourselves, whereto all present felicities afford no resting contentment, will be able at last to tell us we are more than our present selves, and evacuate[44] such hopes in the fruition of their own accomplishments.

¶ *Urn-Burial* Chapter V

Now since these dead bones have already outlasted the living ones of Methuselah,[1] and in a yard underground and thin walls of clay outworn all the strong and specious buildings above it, and quietly rested under the drums and tramplings of three conquests, what prince can promise such diuturnity[2] unto his relics, or might not gladly say, *Sic ego componi versus in ossa velim.*[3] Time which antiquates antiquities and hath an art to make dust of all things hath yet spared these minor monuments. In vain we hope to be known by open and visible conservatories, when to be unknown was the means of their continuation and obscurity their protection. If they died by violent hands, and were thrust into their urns, these bones became considerable, and some old philosophers[4] would honour them, whose souls they conceived most pure which were thus snatched from their bodies, and to retain a stronger propension[5] unto them; whereas they weariedly left a languishing corpse and with faint desires of reunion. If they fell by long and aged decay, yet wrapped up in the bundle of time, they fall into indistinction[6] and make but one blot with infants. If we begin to die

44] annul

1] the oldest person in the Bible, who lived 969 years (Genesis 5:27)   2] long duration   3] 'Thus, I would be buried when I have turned into bones' (Tibullus)   4] Zoroastrian Byzantine writers   5] inclination   6] indistinguishability

when we live, and long life be but a prolongation of death, our life is a sad composition: we live with death and die not in a moment. How many pulses made up the life of Methuselah were work for Archimedes;[7] common counters sum up the life of Moses his man.[8] Our days become considerable like petty sums by minute accumulations, where numerous fractions make up but small round numbers, and our days of a span long make not one little finger.[9]

If the nearness of our last necessity brought a nearer conformity unto it, there were a happiness in hoary hairs and no calamity in half senses. But the long habit of living indisposeth us for dying, when avarice makes us the sport of death,[10] when even David grew politicly cruel,[11] and Solomon could hardly be said to be the wisest of men.[12] But many are too early old, and before the date of age. Adversity stretcheth our days, misery makes Alcmena's nights,[13] and time hath no wings unto it. But the most tedious being is that which can unwish itself, content to be nothing or never to have been, which was beyond the malcontent of Job, who cursed not the day of his life, but his nativity, content to have so far been as to have a title to future being, although he had lived here but in an hidden state of life, and, as it were, an abortion.

What song the sirens sang, or what name Achilles assumed when he hid himself among women,[14] though puzzling questions, are not beyond all conjecture. What time the persons of these ossuaries entered the famous nations of the dead and slept with princes and counsellors might admit a wide solution. But who were the proprietaries of these bones, or what bodies these ashes made up, were a question above antiquarism, not to be resolved by man, nor easily perhaps by spirits, except we consult the provincial guardians or tutelary observators.[15] Had they made as good provision for their names as they have done for their relics, they had not so grossly erred in the art of perpetuation. But to subsist in bones and be but pyramidally extant[16] is a fallacy in

7] who in his *Sand Reckoner* explains how to express very large numbers
8] 'The days of our years are three score years and ten' (Psalm 90:10)
9] in ancient arithmetic the little finger of the right hand signified a hundred
10] our eagerness to retain life makes us especially enticing to death   11] David killed two of every three captured Moabites (2 Samuel 8:2)   12] Solomon in his old age became corrupted by false gods, to whom he built temples (1 Kings 11)   13] 'One night as long as three.' Alcmena, the mother of Hercules by Zeus, endured seven days' labour   14] famous questions put by the emperor Tiberius to test the grammarians (Achilles called himself Pyrrha)   15] guardian angels or tutelary spirits of countries and persons (see *RM* I.33)   16] to exist only in the form of a pyramid tomb

duration; vain ashes, which in the oblivion of names, persons, times, and sexes, have found unto themselves a fruitless continuation, and only arise unto late posterity as emblems of mortal vanities, antidotes against pride, vainglory, and madding vices. Pagan vainglories which thought the world might last forever had encouragement for ambition and, finding no Atropos unto the immortality of their names, were never damped with the necessity of oblivion. Even old ambitions had the advantage of ours in the attempts of their vainglories, who, acting early and before the probable meridian of time,[17] have by this time found great accomplishment of their designs, whereby the ancient heroes have already outlasted their monuments and mechanical preservations.[18] But in this latter scene of time we cannot expect such mummies unto our memories when ambition may fear the prophecy of Elias,[19] and Charles the Fifth can never hope to live within two Methuselahs[20] of Hector.

And therefore restless inquietude for the diuturnity of our memories unto present considerations seems a vanity almost out of date and superannuated piece of folly. We cannot hope to live so long in our names as some have done in their persons; one face of Janus holds no proportion unto the other.[21] 'Tis too late to be ambitious. The great mutations of the world are acted; our time may be too short for our designs. To extend our memories by monuments, whose death we daily pray for, and whose duration we cannot hope without injury to our expectations in the advent of the last day,[22] were a contradiction to our beliefs. We whose generations are ordained in this setting part of time[23] are providentially taken off from such imaginations; and being necessitated to eye the remaining particle of futurity, are naturally constituted unto thoughts of the next world, and cannot excusably decline the consideration of that duration[24] which maketh pyramids pillars of snow and all that's past a moment.

Circles and right lines limit and close all bodies, and the mortal

17] mid-point (i.e. 1000 BC, assuming that the world originated in 4000 BC and will end in AD 2000)   18] manmade protections against decay and spoliation
19] 'That the world may last but six thousand years'   20] Hector's fame has survived two lives of Methuselah (or 1938 years) but since the world was supposed to end in 2000, and Charles was born in 1500, his fame can at best last 500 years   21] the forward-looking face of Janus cannot see as much as the backward-looking one, since time is drawing to a close and there is more past than future to contemplate   22] the Lord's Prayer asks 'Thy Kingdom come', a request which assumes the destruction of all that now is   23] these last days of the world   24] the world to come

right-lined circle[25] must conclude and shut up all. There is no antidote against the opium of time, which temporally considereth all things. Our fathers find their graves in our short memories and sadly tell us how we may be buried in our survivors; gravestones tell truth scarce forty years;[26] generations pass while some trees stand, and old families last not three oaks. To be read by bare inscriptions like many in Gruter, to hope for eternity by enigmatical epithets or first letters of our names,[27] to be studied by antiquaries who we were, and have new names given us like many of the mummies,[28] are cold consolations unto the students of perpetuity, even by everlasting languages.[29]

To be content that times to come should only know there was such a man, not caring whether they knew more of him, was a frigid ambition in Cardan,[30] disparaging his horoscopal inclination[31] and judgement of himself. Who cares to subsist, like Hippocrates' patients or Achilles' horses in Homer, under naked nominations,[32] without desserts and noble acts which are the balsam of our memories, the entelechia[33] and soul of our subsistences? To be nameless in worthy deeds exceeds an infamous history. The Canaanitish woman lives more happily without a name, than Herodias with one.[34] And who had not rather have been the good thief than Pilate?[35]

But the iniquity of oblivion blindly scattereth her poppy, and deals with the memory of men without distinction to merit of perpetuity. Who can but pity the founder of the pyramids? Herostratus lives that burnt the Temple of Diana;[36] he is almost lost that built it; time hath spared the epitaph of Adrian's horse, confounded that of himself. In vain we compute our felicities by the advantage of our good names, since bad have equal durations; and Thersites is like to live as long as Agamemnon. Who knows whether the best of men be known, or whether there be not more remarkable persons forgot than any that

---

25] θ [theta] is the first letter of *thanatos* (death)   26].'Old ones being taken up, and other bodies laid under them'   27] fate or fact construed out of initials   28] 'Which men show in several countries, giving them what names they please; and unto some the names of the old Egyptian kings out of Herodotus.' 29] languages still intelligible to later observers   30] 'I desire it to be known that I am, I do not wish that it be known what sort I am.'   31] his character according to his horoscope   32] in other words to have fame only as a name 33] Aristotelian term for 'soul'   34] the woman who pleaded with Christ to heal her daughter (Matthew 15:22); Herodias asked her father, Herod, for the head of John the Baptist (Matthew 14:8)   35] in Luke (23:43), one of the two malefactors crucified with Christ, who asked to be remembered in the kingdom of heaven; Christ replied, 'Today shalt thou be with me in paradise.'   36] the great temple and Grecian centre of her cult at Ephesus

stand remembered in the known account of time? Without the favour of the everlasting register,[37] the first man had been as unknown as the last, and Methuselah's long life had been his only chronicle.

Oblivion is not to be hired:[38] the greater part must be content to be as though they had not been, to be found in the register of God, not in the record of man. Twenty-seven names make up the first story,[39] and the recorded names ever since contain not one living century.[40] The number of the dead long exceedeth all that shall live. The night of time far surpasseth the day, and who knows when was the equinox?[41] Every hour adds unto that current arithmetic[42] which scarce stands one moment. And since death must be the Lucina[43] of life, and even pagans could doubt whether thus to live were to die; since our longest sun sets at right descensions[44] and makes but winter arches,[45] and therefore it cannot be long before we lie down in darkness, and have our light in ashes, since the brother of death daily haunts us with dying mementoes, and time, that grows old itself, bids us hope no long duration, diuturnity is a dream and folly of expectation.

Darkness and light divide the course of time, and oblivion shares with memory a great part even of our living beings; we slightly remember our felicities, and the smartest strokes of affliction leave but short smart upon us. Sense endureth no extremities, and sorrows destroy us or themselves; to weep into stones are fables;[46] afflictions induce callosities,[47] miseries are slippery, or fall like snow upon us, which notwithstanding is no unhappy stupidity. To be ignorant of evils to come and forgetful of evils past is a merciful provision in nature whereby we digest the mixture of our few and evil days, and, our delivered senses not relapsing into cutting remembrances, our sorrows are not kept raw by the edge of repetitions. A great part of antiquity contented their hopes of subsistency[48] with a transmigration of their souls; a good way to continue their memories, while having the advantage of plural successions, they could not but act something remarkable in such variety of beings, and enjoying the fame of their passed selves, make accumulation of glory unto their last durations. Others,

37] the role of the blessed   38] bribed   39] in the part of Genesis before the flood   40] one hundred   41] the middle point of human history
42] the relentless addition of years onto the sum of human history   43] the goddess of childbirth   44] right angles (i.e. in the summer, when the sun is most directly overhead at noon and the days are longest)   45] winter days (measured by the short path of the sun across the winter sky)   46] perhaps a reference to Niobe, who was said to have turned into a stone while weeping for her dead children.   47] unfeelingness   48] continued existence, continuance

rather than be lost in the uncomfortable night of nothing, were content to recede into the common being, and make one particle of the public soul of all things,[49] which was no more than to return into their unknown and divine original[50] again. Egyptian ingenuity was more unsatisfied, continuing their bodies in sweet consistences[51] to attend the return of their souls. But all was vanity, feeding the wind, and folly. The Egyptian mummies, which Cambyses or time hath spared, avarice now consumeth. Mummy is become merchandise,[52] Mizraim[53] cures wounds, and Pharaoh is sold for balsams.

In vain do individuals hope for immortality or any patent from oblivion[54] in preservations below the moon. Men have been deceived even in their flatteries above the sun, and studied conceits to perpetuate their names in heaven.[55] The various cosmography of that part hath already varied the names of contrived constellations: Nimrod is lost in Orion, and Osiris in the Dog Star. While we look for incorruption in the heavens we find they are but like the earth, durable in their main bodies, alterable in their parts, whereof, beside comets and new stars, perspectives begin to tell tales,[56] and the spots that wander about the sun, with Phaeton's favour,[57] would make clear conviction.

There is nothing strictly immortal but immortality. Whatever hath no beginning may be confident of no end (all others have a dependent being, and within the reach of destruction), which is the peculiar of that necessary essence that cannot destroy itself,[58] and the highest strain of omnipotency to be so powerfully constituted as not to suffer even from the power of itself. But the sufficiency[59] of Christian immortality frustrates all earthly glory, and the quality of either state[60] after death makes a folly of posthumous memory. God, who only can destroy our souls and hath assured our resurrection, either of our bodies or names hath directly promised no duration; wherein there is so much of chance that the boldest expectants have found unhappy frustration; and to hold long subsistence seems but a scape in oblivion.[61]

49] a general world-spirit   50] the chaos of forms   51] i.e. embalmed or mummified with spices   52] the drug mummy, made from mummified bodies, was thought to be sovereign remedy and fetched a high price   53] a generic Egyptian name   54] an indulgence or certificate conferring remission of the sentence of mortality   55] men have attempted to immortalise themselves by having stars named after them   56] telescopes showed that observed phenomena violated the theory of incorruptible crystalline spheres   57] burnt
58] endlessness is a quality of God, who cannot destroy Himself, since it is a characteristic of the greatest of all powers to be powerless against itself
59] adequacy   60] heaven or hell   61] a transgression owing to oversight by oblivion

But man is a noble animal, splendid in ashes and pompous in the grave, solemnizing nativities and deaths with equal lustre, nor omitting ceremonies of bravery in the infamy of his nature.[62]

Life is a pure flame and we live by an invisible sun within us. A small fire sufficeth for life; great flames seemed too little after death while men vainly affected precious pyres, and to burn like Sardanapalus;[63] but the wisdom of funeral laws found the folly of prodigal blazes and reduced undoing fires unto the rule of sober obsequies, wherein few could be so mean as not to provide wood, pitch, a mourner, and an urn.

Five languages secured not the epitaph of Gordianus; the man of God lives longer without a tomb than any by one, invisibly interred by angels and adjudged to obscurity though not without some marks directing human discovery. Enoch and Elias without either tomb or burial, in an anomalous state of being, are the great examples of perpetuity in their long and living memory, in strict account being still on this side death, and having a late part yet to act upon this stage of earth.[64] If in the decretory term[65] of the world we shall not all die but be changed, according to received translation, the last day will make but few graves; at least quick resurrections will anticipate lasting sepultures; some graves will be opened before they be quite closed, and Lazarus be no wonder; when many that feared to die shall groan that they can die but once; the dismal state is the second and living death, when life puts despair on the damned, when men shall wish the coverings of mountains, not of monuments, and annihilation shall be courted.

While some have studied monuments, others have studiously declined them; and some have been so vainly boisterous that they durst not acknowledge their graves, wherein Alaricus seems most subtle, who had a river turned to hide his bones at the bottom. Even Sylla, that thought himself safe in his urn, could not prevent revenging tongues and stones thrown at his monument. Happy are they whom privacy makes innocent, who deal so with men in this world that they are not afraid to meet them in the next, who when they die, make no commotion among the dead, and are not touched with that poetical taunt of Isaiah.[66]

Pyramids, arches, obelisks were but the irregularities of vainglory

---

62] the inherent evil in him   63] who burnt himself and all his household at Nineveh when he could no longer resist the siege he was enduring   64] both ascended alive into heaven, and are therefore not, strictly speaking, dead; both are expected as harbingers of the end of the world   65] decreed limit; i.e. the Last Judgement   66] who prophetically taunted Babylon for its wickedness after the release of the Israelites (Isaiah 14:4-17)

and wild enormities of ancient magnanimity. But the most magnani-
mous resolution rests in the Christian religion, which trampleth upon
pride and sits on the neck of ambition, humbly pursuing that infallible
perpetuity unto which all others must diminish their diameters, and be
poorly seen in angles of contigency.[67]

Pious spirits who passed their days in raptures of futurity made little
more of this world than the world that was before it, while they lay
obscure in the chaos of preordination and night of their forebeings.[68]
And if any have been so happy as truly to understand Christian annihilation, extasis, exolution, liquefaction, transformation, the kiss of
the spouse, gustation of God, and ingression[69] into the divine shadow,
they have already had an handsome anticipation of heaven: the glory
of the world is surely over, and the earth in ashes unto them.

To subsist in lasting monuments, to live in their productions, to
exist in their names and predicament of chimeras[70] was large satisfaction unto old expectations, and made one part of their Elysiums. But
all this is nothing in the metaphysics of true belief. To live indeed is to
be again ourselves, which being not only an hope but an evidence in
noble believers, 'tis all one to lie in St Innocent's churchyard[71] as in the
sands of Egypt, ready to be anything, in the ecstasy of being over, and
as content with six foot as the moles of Adrianus.[72]

Lucan
Tabesne cadavera solvat
An rogus haud refert.[73]

67] 'the least of angles'   68] the chaos which existed before God formed it into
the world; by extension, the embryonic world of the foetus   69] a series of
mystical phrases: extasis, 'ecstasy'; exolution, 'setting free the soul'; liquefaction,
'melting of the soul'; ingression, 'unification'   70] predications made on false
assumptions   71] 'In Paris where bodies soon consume'   72] whose mausoleum has since been built over Castello de St Angelo   73] 'It is unimportant
whether dead bodies are consumed by fire or wither away' (Lucan, *Civil War*)

¶A list of lost curiosities

Musæum Clausum
Antiquities and rarities of several sorts[1]

1. Certain ancient medals with Greek and Roman inscriptions, found about Crim Tartary, conceived to be left in those parts by the soldiers of Mithridates, when, overcome by Pompey, he marched round about the north of the Euxine[2] to come about into Thracia.

2. Some ancient ivory and copper crosses with many others in China, conceived to have been brought and left there by the Greek soldiers who served under Tamerlane in his expedition and conquest of that country.

3. Stones of strange and illegible inscriptions found about the great ruins which Vincent le Blanc describeth about Cephala in Africa, where he opinioned that the Hebrews raised some buildings of old, and that Solomon brought from thereabout a good part of his gold.

4. Some handsome engraveries and medals of Justinus and Justinianus, found in the custody of a banyan[3] in the remote parts of India, conjectured to have been left there by the friars mentioned in Procopius who travelled those parts in the reign of Justinianus and brought back into Europe the discovery of silk and silk worms.

5. An original medal of Petrus Aretinus, who was called *Flagellum Principium*,[4] wherein he made his own figure on the obverse part with this inscription, *Il Divino Aretino*,[5] on the reverse sitting on a throne, and at his feet ambassadors of kings and princes bringing presents unto him, with this inscription,

I Principi tributati da i popoli tributano il servitor loro.[6]

6. *Mummia Tholosana;*[7] or, the complete head and body of Father Crispin, buried long ago in the vault of the Cordeliers at Toulouse,[8] where the skins of the dead so dry and parch up without corruption that their persons may be known very long after, with this inscription,
Ecce iterum Crispinus.[9]

1] *Musæum Clausum*, 'A hidden museum', is a learned parody of such lists of lost antiquities and curiosities; and also of the growing fashion for antiquarian collecting (in which Browne himself, not to mention William Camden, Elias Ashmole and Robert Cotton, took part). The items in *Musæum Clausum* are deliberately obscure (and possibly deliberately incorrect or fanciful in many details) but tantalizing.   2] the Black Sea   3] a Hindu trader   4] 'scourge of the prince'
5] 'The divine Aretino'   6] 'The princes who receive tribute from the people pay tribute to their servant.'   7] The Mummy of Toulouse   8] The Fransiscans of Toulouse apparently sold such mummified or dessicated remains as curios
9] 'Behold Crispin anew'

7. A noble *quandros* or stone taken out of a vulture's head.

8. A large ostrich's egg, whereon is neatly and fully wrought that famous battle of Alcazar, in which three kings lost their lives.[10]

9. An *etiudros Alberti* or stone that is apt to be always moist, useful unto dry tempers, and to be held in the hand in fevers instead of crystal, eggs, lemons, cucumbers.[11]

10. A small vial of water taken out of the stones therefore called *enhydri*,[12] which naturally include a little water in them in like manner as the *aetites* or eagle stone doth another stone.[13]

11. A neat painted and gilded cup made out of the *confiti di Tivoli*[14] and formed with powdered eggshells, as Nero is conceived to have made his *piscina admirabilis*,[15] singular against fluxes[16] to drink often therein.

12. The skin of a snake bred out of the spinal marrow of a man.

13. Vegetable horns mentioned in Linschoten, which set in the ground grow up like plants about Goa.

14. An extract of the ink of cuttlefishes,[17] reviving the old remedy of Hippocrates in hysterical passions.[18]

15. Spirits and salt of Sargasso made in the western ocean,[19] covered with that vegetable; excellent against the scurvy.

16. An extract of *cachunde* or *liberans*,[20] that famous and highly magnified composition in the East Indies against melancholy.

17. *Diarhizon mirificum*,[21] or an unparalleled composition of the most effectual and wonderful roots in nature.

Rx   *Rad. Butuae Cuamensis.*
     Rad. Moniche Cuamensis.
     Rad. Mongus Bazainensis.
     Rad. Casei Bazainensis.
     Rad. Columbae Mozambiguensis.
     Gim. Sem. Sinicae.
     Fo. Lim. lac. Tigridis dictae.
     Fo. seu Cort. Rad. Soldae.

10] either of 1186 or of 1292   11] all presumably thought to draw out the heat of fevers   12] minerals containing water (e.g. certain agates)   13] pebbles of iron oxide clay which have a loose centre. These were said to be found around eagles' nests   14] perhaps a special sweetmeat of Tivoli   15] 'wonderful basin'   16] dysentery and various other intestinal disorders   17] squid   18] psychological symptoms produced by disorders of the uterus   19] a distillation either of gulf-weed, a plant which characteristically floats in the Sargasso Sea, or possibly of the sea-water itself   20]** it is impossible to identify these   21] a 'marvellous emetic'

Rad. Ligni Solorani.

Rad. Malacensis madrededios dictae an. [3] ij.

M. fiat pulvis, qui cum gelatina. Cornu cervi Moschati Chinensis formetur in masas oviformes.[22]

18. A transcendent perfume made of the richest odorates of both the Indies, kept in a box made of the musky[23] stone of Niarienburg, with this inscription,

– Deos rogato
Totum ut te faciant, fabulle, nasum.[24]

19. A *clepselaea*,[25] or oil hourglass, as the ancients used those of water.

20. A ring found in a fish's belly taken about Goro, conceived to be the same wherewith the Duke of Venice had wedded the sea.[26]

21. A neat crucifix made out of the cross-bone of a frog's head.

22. A large agate containing a various and careless[27] figure, which looked upon by a cylinder[28] representeth a perfect centaur. By some such advantages King Pyrrhus might find out Apollo and the nine Muses in those agates of his whereof Pliny maketh mention.

23. *Batrachomyomachia*, or the Homerican battle between frogs and mice, neatly described upon the chizel bone of a large pike's jaw.

24. *Pyxis Pandorae*,[29] or a box which held the *unguentum pestiferum*,[30] which by annointing the garments of several persons begat the great and horrible plague of Milan.[31]

25. A glass of spirits, made of ethereal salt,[32] hermetically sealed up, kept continually in quicksilver; of so volatile a nature that it will scarce endure the light, and therefore only to be shown in winter, or by the light of a carbuncle[33] or Bononian stone.[34]

He who knows where all this treasure now is, is a great Apollo. I'm sure I am not he. However, I am,

Sir, Yours, etc.

Tracts XIII, 116-19

22] this recipe, made mostly of roots, may be a venereal cure   23] musk-scented
24] 'Ask the gods, Fabullus, that they make you all nose' (Catullus)   25] an oil clock which works on the same principle as the clepsydra, a Greek water-clock
26] the Doge of Venice performed an annual ceremony of marriage between the sea and the city in which he threw a ring into the water   27] changeable and [apparently] artless   28] some sort of refracting instrument   29] Pandora's box   30] 'pestilent ointment'   31] in 1630-31   32] volatile salt
33] ruby or garnet   34] phosphorescent sulphate of barium found near Bologna

IV. NATURAL HISTORY

¶Things to be investigated

....Whether it be general that lepers have no lice.

Whether great-eared persons have short necks and long feet, loose bellies.

If in the terraqueous globe all that now is land were sea and all that is sea were land, to discover what great differences there would be in all things as to constitution of climes, tides, navigation, and many other considerables.

Whether in voracious persons and gourmands the distance between the navel and the sternum be greater than from the sternum unto the neck.

An misericordes sint θηλυγόνοι *foemini-genitores,*[1] how verified by your observation and historical example, since pity and mercy are affections of generosity and generous persons are commonly of a masculine temper.

How to make out those physiognomical notes of Aristotle concerning soft and effeminate persons, *genuflexibilitas, inclinatio capitis ad dextram, ambulationes duplices, oculorum circumspectiones.*[2]

Whether halos[3] be so rare betwixt May and September as Gassendus delivereth from his observations in France, and whether his observation there be verified in other climates....

To observe whether animals drowned have no water in their lungs and weasand.[4]

Whether, as there be most female witches, so most females are bewitched, and why?

Whether if observable occurrences[5] were strictly taken notice of

1] 'Whether daughters [or mothers] be compassionate'   2] 'the bowings, the inclination of the head to the right, mincing steps, the eyes glancing about'
3] the refraction of moon- and starlight through atmospheric vapour
4] oesophagus   5] incidents; Browne is suggesting that comets are not special harbingers of unusual events

before the appearing of comets they may not prove as remarkable as those that follow after, an equal space of time being taken before as after....

That if a woman with child looks upon a dead body the child will be pale-complexioned.

That to make urine upon the earth newly cast up by a mole bringeth down the menses.

Why a pig held up by the tail leaves squeaking?....

What is the use of dew claws[6] in dogs?....

To make trial of whether live crawfishes put into spirits of wine will presently turn red as though they had been boiled, and taken out walk about in that colour....

CP 294-300

¶ The cause of thunder

...the cause of those terrible cracks and affrighting noises of heaven...is the nitrous and sulphureous exhalations[1] set on fire in the clouds; whereupon, requiring a larger place, they force out their way not only with the breaking of the cloud but the laceration of the air about it. When if the matter be spiritous[2] and the cloud compact, the noise is great and terrible; if the cloud be thin and the materials weak, the eruption is languid, ending in coruscations and flashes without noise, although but at the distance of two miles, which is esteemed the remotest distance of clouds. And therefore such lightnings do seldom any harm; and therefore also it is prodigious to have thunder in a clear sky, as is observably recorded in some histories.[3]

From the like cause may also proceed subterraneous thunders and earthquakes, when sulphureous and nitreous veins being fired, upon rarefaction do force their way through bodies that resist them. Where if the kindled matter be plentiful, and the mine[4] close and firm about it, subversion of hills and towns doth sometimes follow: if scanty, weak, and the earth hollow or porous, there only ensueth some faint concussion or tremulous quaking motion. Surely, a main reason why

6] rudimentary or false claw above and behind the paw

1] vapours mixed with nitre and sulphur, two ingredients of gunpowder
2] the exhalations of nitre and sulphur are condensed and liquid   3] by Homer, Xenophon, and Cicero   4] any subterranean cavity

the ancients were so imperfect in the doctrine of meteors,[5] was their ignorance of gunpowder and fireworks, which best discover the causes of many thereof.

PE II.v.130-31

¶ Of whispering galleries

....It would be of no small ornament and curiosity to contrive a whispering-place,[1] for if the arching be elliptical, made by a line of double centre denoting the two focuses of the ellipsis, these whispering places may be made. For in the longest diameter of an ellipsis there are two points named the foci, always equidistant from the centre, from one whereof if a line be drawn unto the circumference so reflecting that the angle of reflection be equal unto that of incidence, they will reflect unto the other focus, and so the sound be conveyed unto him whose ear lieth at it. And therefore if we whisper at one focus, all the vocal rays which are carried unto the circumference of the ellipsis are by reflection all united in the other focus, and by the multitude and union of these reflexed rays the voice be strongly heard at the other extreme or focus, not easily in the middle, unto which one direct and single ray only arriveth.

Nor to rest in the bare architect or fabric,[2] but upon the same to inscribe the mechanical draught[3] wherein lie the causes and reasons of this admirable effect, the figure being drawn in red or blue extending the whole length of the arch, and each focus denoted by some mark or special colour whereat may stand two figures of Cupids, boys or handsome draughts with the mouth to one focus, the ear unto the other, according to this draught (the rule) which containeth the mystery[4] of this effect.

Near the same in other spaces may be drawn the best acoustic instruments contrived for advantage of hearing, such as may be seen in Bellini's.

Notes 242-3

5] atmospheric phenomena

1] a whispering gallery   2] not to let the structure remain bare of decoration or embellishment ['architect'** for 'architecture']   3] emphasis of the structural features by decoration with lines and colours   4] the secret

¶ Of bodies electrical

....No metal attracts, nor animal concretion we know, although polite[1]
and smooth, as we have made trial in elk's hoofs, hawk's talons, the
swordfish of a swordfish, tortoise shells, seahorse, and elephant's teeth, in
bones, in hartshorn, and what is usually conceived unicorn's horn. No
wood, though never so hard and polished, although out of some
thereof electric bodies[2] proceed, as ebony, box, *lignum vitae*,[3] cedar,
etc. And although jet and amber be reckoned among bitumens, yet
neither do we find *asphaltus*,[4] that is, bitumens of Judea, nor sea coal,
nor camphor, nor *mummia*[5] to attract, although we have tried in large
and polished pieces. Now this attraction have we tried in straws and
paleous[6] bodies, in needles of iron equilibriated, powders of wood and
iron, in gold and silver foliate.[7] And not only in solid but fluent and
liquid bodies, as oils made both by expression[8] and distillation, in
water, in spirits of wine, vitriol[9] and *aqua fortis*.[10]

But how this attraction is made is not so easily determined. That 'tis
performed by effluviums[11] is plain, and granted by most, for electrics
will not commonly attract, except they grow hot or become
perspirable.[12] For if they be foul and obnubilated,[13] it hinders their
effluxion,[14] nor if they be covered, though but with linen or sarsenet,[15]
or if a body be interposed, for that intercepts the effluvium. If also a
powerful and broad electric of wax or anime[16] be held over fine powder, the atoms or small particles will ascend most numerously unto it;
and if the electric be held unto the light, it may be observed that many
thereof will fly, and be as it were discharged from the electric to the
distance sometime of two or three inches, which motion is performed
by the breath of the effluvium issuing with agility; for as the electric
cooleth, the projection of the atoms ceaseth.

The manner hereof Cabeus wittily attempteth, affirming that this
effluvium attenuateth and impelleth the neighbour air, which returning home in a gyration, carrieth with it the obvious bodies unto the

---

1] polished (from L. *polire*)   2] charged with electricity. TB: 'By electric bodies,
I conceive...such as conveniently placed unto their objects attract all bodies palpa-
ble.'   3] ebony or cedar   4] smooth, brittle mixture of various hydrocarbons
5] medicine made from the bituminous remains of mummified bodies
6] chaffy   7] beaten into foil   8] squeezing   9] sulphuric acid or sulphate
of iron   10] nitric acid   11] outflowing particles too subtle to be perceived
by the senses   12] able to be blown through, or capable of being thrown off in
perspiration   13]** clouded (from 'nubliated')   14] out-flow of particles
15] very fine silk   16] a kind of resin

electric. And this he labours to confirm by experiments; for if the straws be raised by a vigorous electric, they do appear to wave and turn in their ascents. If likewise the electric be broad, and the straws light and chaffy, and held at a reasonable distance, they will not arise unto the middle, but rather adhere toward the verge or borders thereof. And lastly, if many straws be laid together, and a nimble electric approach, they will not all arise unto it, but some will commonly start aside and be whirled a reasonable distance from it. Now that the air impelled returns unto its place in a gyration or whirling is evident from the atoms or motes in the sun. For when the sun so enters a hole or window, that by its illumination the atoms or motes become perceptible, if then by our breath the air be gently impelled, it may be perceived that they will circularly return and in a gyration unto their places again....

PE II.iv.118-19

¶ Of the loadstone

...It is also improbable and something singular what some conceive, and Eusebius Nierembergius, a learned Jesuit of Spain delivers, that the body of man is magnetical, and being placed in a boat, the vessel will never rest until the head respecteth[1] the north. If this be true, the bodies of Christians do lie unnaturally in their graves.[2] King Cheops in his tomb, and the Jews in their beds have fallen upon the natural position, who, reverentially declining the situation of their temple, nor willing to lie as that stood, do place their beds from north to south and delight to sleep meridionally.[3] This opinion confirmed would much advance the microcosmical conceit[4] and commend the geography of Paracelsus, who according to the cardinal points of the world[5] divideth the body of man; and therefore working upon human ordure, and by long preparation rendering it odiferous,[6] he terms it *zibeta occidentalis*, western civet;[7] making the face the east, but the posteriors the America or western part of his microcosm. The verity hereof might easily be tried in Wales, where there are portable boats, and made of

1] faces   2] because Christians in ancient tradition were buried with their heads toward the west   3] along a north-south line   4] the idea that the structure of the human body is in some sense a mirror or a copy of that of the world
5] the four points of the compass   6] fragrant   7] substance used in perfumery derived from the anal glands of the civet-cat of Africa and Asia

leather, which would convert upon the impulsion of any verticity;[8] and seem to be the same whereof in his description of Britain Caesar hath left some mention....

Many other magnetisms may be pretended, and the like attractions through all the creatures of nature. Whether the same be verified in the action of the sun upon inferior bodies, whether there be Aeolian magnets,[9] whether the flux and reflux of the sea be caused by any magnetism from the moon, whether the like be really made out, or rather metaphorically verified, in the sympathies of plants and animals,[10] might afford a large dispute....

Other discourses there might be made of loadstone, as moral, mystical, theological;[11] and some have handsomely done them; as Ambrose, Austin, Gulielmus Parisiensis, and many more; but these fall under no rule, and are as boundless as men's inventions. And though honest minds do glorify God hereby, yet do they most powerfully magnify him, and are to be looked on with another eye, who demonstratively set forth its magnalities,[12] who not from postulated or precarious inferences, entreat a courteous assent, but from experiments and undeniable effects enforce the wonder of its maker.

PE II.iii.105-16

¶ Of swimming and floating

...that persons drowned arise and float the ninth day when their gall breaketh[1] is a questionable determination both in the time and cause. For the time of floating, it is uncertain according to the time of putrefaction, which shall retard or accelerate according to the subject and season of year, for as we have observed, cats and mice will arise unequally, and at different times, though drowned at the same. Such as are fat do commonly float soonest, for their bodies soonest ferment, and that substance approacheth nearest unto air;[2] and this is one of

---

8] tendency to turn toward the vertex or pole   9] magnetical forces which produce winds   10] selenotropic and heliotropic plants and animals are not magnetically, but sympathetically, attracted to the moon and sun   11] symbolical interpretations of magnetical attraction have yielded moral, mystical, and theological explanations of it   12]* great and wonderful things

1] the accumulation of gases in the corpse, especially in the gall bladder, forces it to the surface   2] in Aristotle's theory of matter, the tendency of fat is to rise because it is 'airy'

Aristotle's reasons why dead eels will not float, because saith he, they have but slender bellies, and little fat....

That the breaking of the gall is not the cause hereof, experience hath informed us, for opening the abdomen, and taking out the gall in cats and mice, they did notwithstanding arise. And because we had read in Rhodiginus of a tyrant, who to prevent the emergency[3] of murdered bodies did use to cut off their lungs, and found men's minds possessed with this reason, we committed some unto water without lungs, which notwithstanding floated with the others. And to complete the experiment, although we took out the guts and bladder, and also perforated the cranium, yet would they arise, though in a longer time. From these observations in other animals it may not be unreasonable to conclude the same in man, who is too noble a subject on whom to make them expressly, and the casual opportunity too rare almost to make any. Now if any should ground this effect from gall or choler, because it is the highest humour[4] and will be above the rest, or being the fiery humour will readiest surmount the water, we must confess in the common putrescence it may promote elevation, which the breaking of the bladder of gall, so small a part in man, cannot considerably advantage.

Lastly, that women drowned float prone, that is, with their bellies downward, but men supine or upward, is an assertion wherein the *hoti*[5] or point itself is dubious; and were it true, the reason alleged for it is of no validity. The reason yet current was first expressed by Pliny: *veluti pudori defunctorum parcente natura*, 'nature modestly ordaining this position to conceal the shame of the dead'; which hath been taken up by Solinus, Rhodiginus, and many more. This indeed (as Scaliger termeth it) is *ratio civilis non philosophica*,[6] strong enough for morality of rhetorics, not for philosophy or physics.[7] For first, in nature the concealment of secret parts is the same in both sexes, and the shame of their reveal equal; so Adam upon the taste of the fruit was ashamed of his nakedness as well as Eve. And so, likewise, in America and countries unacquainted with habits,[8] where modesty conceals these parts in one sex, it doth also in the other; and therefore, had this been the intention of nature, not only women but men also had swimmed downwards, the posture in reason being common unto both where the intent is also common....

3] emergence   4] choler or bile (produced in the gall bladder); responsible for irascibility, and associated with fire   5] an assertion of fact   6] 'a social, but not philosophical, reason'   7] natural sciences   8] clothes

That a mare will sooner drown than a horse, though commonly opinioned, is not, I fear, experienced; nor is the same observed in the drowning of whelps and kitlins. But that a man cannot shut or open his eyes under water easy experiment may convict.[9] Whether cripples and mutilated persons, who have lost the greatest part of their thighs, will not sink but float, their lungs being abler to waft up their bodies, which are in others overpoised by the hinder legs, we have not made experiment. Thus much we observe, that animals drown downwards, and the same is observable in frogs, when the hinder legs are cut off. But in the air[10] most seem to perish headlong from high place (however Vulcan, thrown from heaven, be made to fall on his feet).

PE IV.vi.287-90

¶ Of spermaceti, and the spermaceti whale.

What spermaceti[1] is men might justly doubt, since the learned Hofmannus, in his work of thirty years,[2] saith plainly, *Nescio quid sit*,[3] and therefore need not wonder at the variety of opinions, while some conceived it to be *flos maris*,[4] and many, a bituminous substance floating upon the sea.

That it was not the spawn of the whale, according to vulgar conceit or nominal appellation, philosophers have always doubted, not easily conceiving the seminal humour of animals should be inflammable or of a floating nature.

That it proceedeth from a whale, beside the relation of Clusius and other learned observers, was indubitably determined, not many years since by a spermaceti whale cast on our coast of Norfolk which, to lead on further enquiry, we cannot omit to inform. It contained no less than sixty foot in length, the head somewhat peculiar, with a large prominency over the mouth; teeth only in the lower jaw, received into fleshly sockets in the upper, the weight of the largest about two pound; no gristly substances in the mouth, commonly called whalebones;[5] only two short fins seated forwardly on the back; the eyes but

1] a waxy substance found in the head and blubber of the sperm whale; it was used medicinally and in the manufacture of very superior candles; the name ('sperm of the whale') suggests the mistaken notion of its origin which Browne here refutes   2] *De Medicamentis Officinalibus* (1647)   3] 'I do not know what it is'   4] a sea plant   5] baleen, the cartilaginous bones of the mouth

small; the pizzel[6] large and prominent. A lesser whale of this kind above twenty years ago was cast upon the same shore.

The description of this whale seems omitted by Gesner, Rondeletius, and the first editions of Aldrovandus, but described in the Latin impression of Pareus, in the *Exoticks* of Clusius, and the *Natural History* of Nirembergius; but more amply in icons[7] and figures of Johnstonus.

Mariners (who are not the best nomenclators)[8] called it a *jubartas*, or rather *gibbartas*.[9] Of the same appellation we meet with one in Rondeletius, called by the French *gibbar*, from its round and gibbous[10] back. The name *gibbarta* we find also given unto one kind of Greenland whales, but this of ours seemed not to answer the whale of that denomination, but was more agreeable unto the *trumpa* or spermaceti whale according to the account of our Greenland describers in Purchas, and maketh the third among the eight remarkable whales of that coast.

Out of the head of this whale, having been dead divers days and under putrefaction, flowed streams of oil and spermaceti which was carefully taken up and preserved by the coasters. But upon breaking up, the magazine[11] of spermaceti was found in the head lying in folds and courses in the bigness of goose eggs, encompassed with large flaxy substances as large as a man's head in form of honeycombs, very white and full of oil.

Some resemblance or trace hereof there seems to be in the physiter or *capidolio*[12] of Rondeletius, while he delivers that a fatness more liquid than oil runs from the brain of that animal, which being out, the relics are like the scales of sardinos pressed into a mass, which melting with heat, are again concreted by cold. And this many conceive to have been the fish which swallowed Jonas, although for the largeness of the mouth and frequency in those seas, it may possibly be the *lamia*.[13]

Some part of the spermaceti found on the shore was pure and needed little depuration;[14] a great part mixed with fetid oil, needing good preparation, and frequent expression to bring it to a flaky consistency. And not only the head, but other parts contained it; for the carnous parts being roasted, the oil dropped out, an axungious[15] and

6] penis   7] illustrations   8] scientific name-givers (the lack of technical classification of animals is a central concern of Browne's)   9] the rorqual or finwhale, also known as a gibbert   10] humped   11] store-house
12]** Greek and Italian names for one of the toothed whales   13] the white shark   14] purification or refining   15] greasy

thicker part subsiding; the oil itself contained also much in it, and still after many years some is obtained from it.[16]

Greenland enquirers seldom meet with a whale of this kind, and therefore it is but a contingent commodity, not reparable[17] from any other. It flameth white and candent[18] like camphor, but dissolveth not in *aqua fortis*, like it. Some lumps containing about two ounces, kept ever since in water, afford a fresh and flosculous[19] smell. Well prepared and separated from the oil, it is of a substance unlikely to decay, and may outlast the oil required in the composition of Mathiolus.[20]

Of the large quantity of oil, what first came forth by expression from the spermaceti grew very white and clear, like that of almonds or ben.[21] What came by decoction[22] was red. It was found to spend[23] much in the vessels which contained it. It freezeth or coagulateth quickly with cold, and the newer soonest. It seems different from the oil of any other animal, and very much frustrated the expectation of our soap-boilers, as not incorporating or mingling with their lyes. But it mixeth well with painting colours, though hardly drieth at all. Combers of wool[24] made use hereof, and country people for cuts, aches and hard tumours. It may prove of good medical[25] use, and serve for a ground in compounded oils and balsams.[26] Distilled, it affords a strong oil with a quick and piercing water.[27] Upon evaporation it gives a balsam, which is better performed[28] with turpentine distilled with spermaceti.

Had the abominable scent permitted, enquiry had been made into that strange composure of the head, and hillock of flesh about it. Since the workmen affirmed they met with spermaceti before they came to the bone, and the head yet preserved, seems to confirm the same[29]....The heart, lungs, and kidneys had not escaped,[30] wherein are remarkable differences from animals of the land; likewise, what humour the bladder contained, but especially the seminal parts, which

16] the waxy spermaceti and the blubber cooked together yield sperm oil, used as a lubricant. By chilling this, spermaceti could be made to congeal out of it. The arduous process of deriving the sperm oil from the flesh and blubber of the whale, and then of separating the spermaceti from it, is described in *Moby Dick* by Melville, who was much influenced by Browne's account of capturing the various substances of the sperm whale   17] available   18] glowing white   19]* flowery 20] oil a hundred years old was specified as an ingredient in a remedy described by Pietro Mattioli   21] horse-radish seed   22] extraction by boiling 23] be destroyed or wasted   24] wool carders   25]* Browne's neologism 26] healing ointments   27] rapid-acting and effective medicinal preparation 28] accomplished   29] that spermaceti is also found in the large hump on the head of the whale   30] did not survive to be examined might have determined the difference of that humour[31] from this which beareth its name.

In vain it was to rake for ambergris[32] in the paunch of this leviathan, as Greenland discovers and attests[33] of experience dictate that they sometimes swallow great lumps thereof in the sea, insufferable fetour[34] denying that enquiry. And yet if, as Paracelsus encourageth, ordure makes the best musk,[35] and from the most fetid substances may be drawn the most odiferous essences, all that had not Vespasian's nose[36] might boldly swear here was a subject fit for such extractions.

PE III.xxvi.251-4

¶ Of the kingfisher

That a kingfisher hanged by the bill showeth in what quarter the wind is by an occult and secret propriety,[1] converting the breast to that point of the horizon from whence the wind doth blow, is a received opinion, and very strange, introducing natural weathercocks and extending magnetical positions as far as animal natures, a conceit supported chiefly by present practice, yet not made out by reason or experience.

Unto reason it seemeth very repugnant that a carcass, or body disanimated,[2] should be so affected with every wind as to carry a comfortable respect and constant habitude thereto.[3] For although in sundry animals we deny not a kind of natural meteorology or innate presention[4] both of wind and weather, yet that proceeding from sense, receiving impressions from the first mutation of the air, they cannot in reason retain that apprehension after death, as being affections which depend on life and depart upon disanimation. And therefore with more favourable reason may we draw the same effect or sympathy upon the hedgehog, whose presention of winds is so exact that it stoppeth the north or southern hole of its nest according to the

31] semen   32] a valuable intestinal secretion of the sperm whale found floating in tropical seas; used in perfumery and cookery; it was thought that whales swallowed ambergris, not that they produced it   33] testimonies   34] stench
35] true musk is made from the secretions of the anal sac of certain animals, whence the term 'ordure'   36] who responded to his son's complaint about his policy of collecting taxes on the urinals of Rome with the remark *pecunia non olet* ('money doesn't smell')

1] a mystical and hidden conformity between the kingfisher and the wind
2] unsouled   3] behave in accordance with it   4]** foreknowledge

prenotion[5] of these winds ensuing, which some men observing have been able to make predictions which way the wind would turn, and been esteemed hereby wise men in point of weather. Now this proceeding from sense in the creature alive, it were not reasonable to hang up a hedgehog's head and to expect a conformable motion unto its living conversion.[6] And though in sundry plants their virtues do live after death, and we know that scammony, rhubarb and senna[7] will purge[8] without any vital asistance,[9] yet in animals and sensible creatures many actions are mixed, and depend upon their living form as well as that of mistion;[10] and though they wholly seem to retain unto the body,[11] depart upon disunion. Thus glowworms alive project a lustre in the dark, which fulgour,[12] notwithstanding, ceaseth after death; and thus the torpedo, which being alive stupefies at a distance, applied after death produceth no such effect, which, had they retained in places where they abound, they might have supplied opium, and served as frontals in frenzies.[13]

As for experiment, we cannot make it out by any we have attempted; for if a single kingfisher be hanged up with untwisted silk in an open room and where the air is free, it observes not a constant respect unto the mouth of the wind, but variously converting doth seldom breast it right.[14] If two be suspended in the same room they will not regularly conform their breasts, but ofttimes respect the opposite points of heaven. And if we conceive that for exact exploration[15] they should be suspended where the air is quiet and unmoved, that clear of impediments they may more freely convert upon their natural verticity,[16] we have also made this way of inquisition, suspending them in large and capacious glasses closely stopped, wherein nevertheless we observed a casual station,[17] and that they rested irregularly upon conversion; wheresoever they rested, remaining inconverted and possessing one point of the compass whilst the wind perhaps had passed the two and thirty.[18]

The ground of this popular practice might be the common opinion concerning the virtue prognostic[19] of these birds, as also the natural

5] foreknowledge   6] a similar tendency to predict winds when dead because it did so alive   7] purgative plants   8] produce vomiting, a standard medical treatment of the time   9] without being themselves still alive   10] mixture 11] be a feature of the physical (not the mental) aspect of the animal 12] brightness   13] medicines applied to the head to cure manias and deliriums 14] point to the correct quarter   15] precise measurement   16] tendency to turn toward a vertex or pole   17] random position at rest   18] i.e. into another quarter altogether   19] the premonitory ability

regard they have unto the winds, and they unto them[20] again, more especially remarkable in the time of their nidulation[21] and bringing forth their young. For at that time, which happeneth about the brumal[22] solstice, it hath been observed even unto a proverb that the sea is calm and the winds do cease till the young ones are excluded;[23] and forsake their nest which floateth upon the sea, and by the roughness of winds might otherwise be overwhelmed. But how far hereby to magnify their prediction we have no certain rule, for whether out of any particular prenotion they choose to sit at this time, or whether it be thus contrived by concurrence of causes and providence of nature securing every species in their production, is not yet determined. Surely many things fall out by the design of the general motor[24] and undreamt-of contrivance of nature which are not imputable unto the intention or knowledge of the particular actor....So if, as Pliny and Plutarch report, the crocodiles of Egypt so aptly lay their eggs that the natives thereby are able to know how high the flood[25] will attain, it will be hard to make out how they should divine the extent of the inundation depending on causes so many miles remote (that is, the measure of showers in Ethiopia), and whereof, as Athanasius in the life of Anthony delivers, the devil himself upon demand could make no clear prediction. So are there likewise many things in nature which are the forerunners or signs of future effects, whereto they neither concur in causality or prenotion, but are secretly ordered by the providence of causes, and concurrence of actions collateral to their signations.[26]

PE III.x.186-9

¶ Of the badger

That a brock or badger hath the legs on one side shorter than of the other, though an opinion perhaps not very ancient, is yet very general, received not only by theorists and unexperienced believers, but assented unto by most who have the opportunity to behold and hunt them daily. Which notwithstanding, upon enquiry I find repugnant unto the three determinators of truth – authority, sense, and reason.

20] the winds to the birds   21] nesting   22] winter   23] turned out of the nest   24] the universal motivating force of nature   25] the annual flooding of the Nile, said to be predictable in its height by the level on the banks at which crocodiles laid their eggs   26]* predictions whose distinctive phenomena bear no apparent similitude to the things predicted

For first, Albertus Magnus speaks dubiously, confessing he could not confirm the verity hereof; but Aldrovandus plainly affirmeth there can be no such inequality observed. And for my own part, upon indifferent enquiry, I cannot discover this difference, although the regardable side be defined, and the brevity by most imputed unto the left.

Again, it seems no easy affront unto reason, and generally repugnant unto the course of nature; for if we survey the total set of animals, we may in their legs or organs of progression observe an equality of length and parity of numeration; that is, not any to have an odd leg, or the supporters and movers of one side not exactly answered by the other. Although the hinder may be unequal to the fore and middle legs, as in frogs, locusts, and grasshoppers; or both unto the middle, as in some beetles and spiders, as is determined by Aristotle (*De incessu Animalium*). Perfect and viviparous[1] quadrupeds so standing in their position of proneness that the opposite joints of neighbour legs consist in the same plane, and a line descending from their navel intersects at right angles the axis of the earth. It happeneth often, I confess, that a lobster hath the chely or great claw of one side longer than the other, but this is not properly their leg, but a part of apprehension,[2] and whereby they hold or seize upon their prey; for the legs and proper parts of progression are inverted backward, and stand in a position opposite unto these.

Lastly, the monstrosity[3] is ill contrived, and with some disadvantage, the shortness being affixed unto the legs of one side, which might have been more tolerably placed upon the thwart or diagonial movers. For the progression of quadrupeds being performed *per diametrum* – that is, the cross legs moving or resting together, so that two are always in motion and two in station at the same time – the brevity had been more tolerable in the cross legs. For then the motion and station had been performed by equal legs, whereas herein they are both performed by unequal organs, and the imperfection becomes discoverable at every hand.

PE III.v.170-71

1] born fully developed   2] the member with which they 'apprehend' or take
hold   3] abnormality

¶ Of beavers

....Camden reports that in former time there have been beavers in the river of Cardigan in Wales. This we are too sure of, that the rivers, great broads, and cars[1] afford great store of otters with us, a great destroyer of fish, as feeding but from the vent[2] downwards; not free from being a prey itself, for their young ones have been found in buzzards' nests. They are accounted no bad dish by many, are to be made very tame, and in some houses have served for turnspits.[3]

Notes 426

¶ The wisdom of ants

....The wisdom of the pismire is magnified by all, and in the panegyricks of their providence we always meet with this, that to prevent the growth of corn which they store up, they bite off the end thereof; and some have conceived that from hence they have their name in Hebrew;[1] from whence ariseth a conceit that corn will not grow if the extremes be cut or broken. But herein we find no security to prevent its germination, as having made trial in grains whose ends cut off have, notwithstanding, suddenly sprouted, and accordingly to the law of their kinds; that is, the roots of barley and oats at contrary ends, of wheat and rye at the same. And therefore some have delivered that after rainy weather they dry these grains in the sun, which, if effectual, we must conceive to be made in a high degree and above the progression of malt; for that malt will grow, this year hath informed us,[2] and that unto a perfect ear.

And if that be true which is delivered by many, (and we shall further experiment) that a decoction of toadstools if poured upon earth, will produce the same again, if sow-thistles will abound in places manured with dung of hogs, which feeds much upon that plant, if horse-dung reproduceth oats, if winds and rains will transport the seminals[3] of plants, it will not be easy to determine where the power of generation ceaseth. The forms of things may lie deeper than we conceive them; seminal principles may not be dead in the divided atoms of plants, but

1] bogs or fens   2] anus   3] animals (usually small dogs) harnessed to the spits to rotate meat during cooking

1] according to Browne, *Nemalah a Namal circumcidit* (Proverbs. 6:6: 'Go to the ant, thou sluggard; consider her ways, and be wise.')   2] 1645   3] seeds

wandering in the ocean of nature, when they hit upon proportionable
materials,[4] may unite and return to their visible selves again.

But the prudence of this animal is by gnawing, piercing, or otherwise to destroy the little neb[5] or principle of germination; which notwithstanding is not easily discoverable, it being no ready business to
meet with such grains in anthills; and he must dig deep, that will seek
them in winter.

PE III.xxvii.263-4

¶Animal antipathies

Many antipathies are delivered which are not, and even when they are
verified they do but vex us with the poverty of their solutions.

There is delivered us one unto the viper, whereof I could never see
a clear conviction; of spiders and toads we have elsewhere spoken thus
much at present. We intered a mole, a toad, and a viper in one glass;
within half an hour the mole eat up half the viper leaving the tail and
harder parts, destroyed the toad, eat part of the entrails, died the next
day...which I imputed not unto so...large a meal, for they will not
commonly live above a day or two out of the earth....

The antipathy between a toad and a spider, and that they
poisonously destroy each other, is very famous, and solemn stories
have been written of their combats, wherein most commonly the victory is given unto the spider. Of what toads and spiders it is to be
understood would be considered, for the *phalangium*[1] and deadly
spiders are different from those we generally behold in England. However, the verity hereof, as also of many others, we cannot but desire;
for hereby we might be surely provided of proper antidotes in cases
which require them. But what we have observed herein, we cannot in
reason conceal, who having in a glass included a toad with several
spiders, we beheld the spiders without resistance to sit upon his head
and pass over all his body, which at last upon advantage he swallowed
down, and that in a few hours, unto the number of seven. And in the
like manner will toads also serve bees, and are accounted enemies unto
their hives.

Notes 366;
PE III.xxvii.258-9

4] nutrients   5] the embryo of a seed

1] a venomous spider (Greek)

¶ Observations of the ostrich

The ostrich hath a compounded name in Greek and Latin, *struthio-camelus*,[1] borrowed from a bird and a beast as being a feathered and biped animal, yet in some ways like a camel, somewhat in the long neck, somewhat in the foot, and as some imagine, from a camel-like position in the part of generation.

It is accounted the largest and tallest of any winged and feathered fowl, taller than the emu or cassowary. This ostrich,[2] though a female, was above seven foot high, and some of the males were higher, either exceeding or answerable unto the stature of the great porter unto King Charles the First.[3] The weight was a *quaere* or try[4] in grocer's scales.

Whosoever shall compare or consider together the ostrich and the tomineio, or humbird, not weighing twelve grains,[5] may easily discover under what compass or latitude[6] the creation of birds hath been ordained.

The head is not large, but little in proportion to the whole body. And therefore Julius Scaliger, when he mentioneth birds of large heads comparatively unto their bodies, nameth the sparrow, the owl and the woodpecker; and, reckoning up birds of small heads, instanceth in the hen, the peacock, and the ostrich.

The head is looked upon by discerning spectators to resemble that of a goose, rather than any kind of στρουθος [7] or passere,[8] and so it may be more properly called the *cheno-camelus* or *ansero-camelus*.[9]

There is a handsome figure of an ostrich in Mr Willoughby's and Mr Ray's *Ornithologia*, another in Aldrovandus and Johnstonus and Bellonius, but the heads not exactly agreeing. *Rostrum habet exiguum sed acutum*,[10] saith Johnstonus; *un long bec et pointu*,[11] saith Bellonius, men describing such as they have an opportunity to see, and perhaps some of the ostriches of very distant countries, wherein, as in some other birds, there may be some variety...

When it first came into my garden it soon eat up all the gilliflowers,

1] ostriches belong to the order *struthioformes*   2] Browne had kept an ostrich at some point before his son Edward acquired one in 1682   3] Sir John Millicent, who played Goliath and other giant roles in masques for James I
4] an unanswered question (probably because the scales were not big enough to weigh the ostrich)   5] the tomin was a jeweller's measure of gold, equal to twelve grains or about three carats   6] expanse or breadth of variety
7] 'strouthos'   8] a large genus of perching birds   9] 'goose-footed-camel'; 'camel grey-goose'   10] 'It has a short but sharp bill'   11] 'a long and pointed beak'

tulip leaves, and fed greedily upon what was green, as lettuce, endive, sorrel: it would feed upon oats, barley, pease, beans, swallow onions, eat sheep's lights[12] and livers...

When it took down a large onion it stuck awhile in the *gula*[13] and did not descend directly, but wound backward behind the neck, whereby I might perceive that the gullet turned much; but this is not peculiar unto the ostrich, but the same hath been observed in the stork when it swallows down frogs and pretty big bits.

It made sometimes a strange noise, had a very odd note, especially in the morning and perhaps when hungry.

According to Aldrovandus, some hold that there is an antipathy between it an[d] a horse, which an ostrich will not endure to see or be near, but while I kept it I could not confirm this opinion, which might perhaps be raised because a common way of hunting and taking them is by swift horses.

It is much that Cardanus should be mistaken with a great part of men that the coloured and dyed feathers of ostriches were natural, as red, blue, narrow[14] green, whereas the natural colours in this bird were white and greyish. If fashion of wearing feathers in hats and headpieces by men, and of women...wearing of feather fans should come up again, it might much increase the trade of plumage from Barbary. Bellonius saith he saw two hundred skins with feathers on in one shop of Alexandria.

In Africa, where some eat elephants, it is no wonder that some also feed upon ostriches. They flay them with the feathers on, which they sell, and eat the flesh, but Galen and physicians have condemned that flesh as hardly digestible, and therefore when according to Lampridius the Emperor Heliogabalus forced the Jews to eat ostriches, it was a meat not only of hard digestion to their stomachs, but also to the consciences, as being a forbidden meat food. The Emperor Heliogabalus had a fancy for the brains when he brought six hundred ostrich heads to one supper only for the brains' sake, yet Leo Africanus saith that he eat of young ostriches among the Numidians with a good gust. And perhaps boiled and well cooked after the art of Apicius, with peppermint, dates, and other good things, they might go down with some stomachs.

I do not find that the strongest eagles or best spirited hawks will offer at these birds, yet if there were such gerfalcons as Julius Scaliger saith the Duke of Savoy and King of Navarre had, 'tis like they would

12] lungs   13] gullet   14]** not recorded in OED

strike at them, and making at the head would spoil them or so disable them that they might be taken.

If these had been brought over in June, 'tis perhaps like we might have met with eggs in some of their bellies, whereof they lay very many; but they are the worst of eggs for food, yet serviceable unto many other uses in their country, for being cut transversely they serve for drinking cups, and skull-caps, and as I have seen, there are large circles of them, and some painted and gilded, which hang up in Turkish mosques and also in Greek churches. They are preserved with us for rarities, and if they come to be common some use will be found of them in physic, even as of other eggshells and other such substances.

Notes 354-6

¶ King Charles's ostriches (to Edward Browne)

Jan 13 [1681-2]

D.s.,[1]

I thank you for the account of the ambassador of the King of Fez and Morocco. You did well to give a visit unto a person so unusual and so much talked of. He will at his return tell stories of wonder unto his countrymen, and such as they will hardly understand, but I think the King doth wisely to caress him and show him the respect he giveth him, for such a tyrannical ambitious prince as he serveth may probably be sooner taken with such honours than with ordinary respects ....There being so many ostriches brought over 'tis likely some of them will [be] brought about to show, and hither as soon as other parts out of London. If any of them die, I believe it will be dissected. They have odd feet and strong thighs and legs. 'Tis much[2] the use of the eggshells is not more common in physic, like other eggshells and crabs' eyes or claws, and there would be enough to be had if they were looked after and sought for by the drugsters. Perhaps the King will put three or four of these ostriches into St James's Park and give away the rest to some noblemen...

Letters 204-05

1] 'Dear son'   2] odd, inexplicable

¶ Practical ostrich-keeping (to Edward Browne)

Feb 3 [1681-2]
D.S.,
I believe you must be careful of your ostrich[1] this return [of] cold
weather, lest it perish by it being bred in so hot a country and perhaps
not seen snow before or very seldom; so that I believe it must be kept
under cover and have straw to sit upon and water set by it to take of
both day and night; must have it observed how it sleepeth and whether
not with the head under the wing, especially in cold weather; whether
it be a watchful and quick-hearing bird like a goose, for it seems to be
like a goose in many circumstances. It seems to eat anything that a
goose will feed on, and like a goose to love the same green herbs and
to delight in lettuce, endive, sorrel, etc. You will be much at a loss for
herbs this winter, but you may have cheap and easy supply by cab-
bages, which I forgot to mention in my last, and drains,[2] all kind of
grains and bran, or furfures,[3] alone or mixed with water or other liquor. To geese they give oats, etc. moistened with beer, but sometimes
they are inebriated with it. If you give any iron, it may be wrapped up
in dough or paste; perhaps it will not take it up alone. You may try
whether it will eat a worm or a very small eel; whether it will drink
milk; and observe in what manner it drinks water. Aldrovandus and
Johnstonus write that a goose will not eat bay leaves and that they are
bad for it. You may lay a bay leaf by the ostrich and observe whether it
will take it up. You may in your next draw the figure of the head with
a pen, for the icons in Bellonius, Johnstonus, and Aldrovandus do not
seem to be strictly like yours. When it is anatomized, I suppose the
skeleton will be made[4] and you may stuff the skin with the feathers
on...When the dissection of it is intended, it were fit to take the weight
of it. If it delights not in salt things you may try it with an olive....The
King or gentlemen will be little taken with the anatomy of it,[5] though
that must also be, but are like to take more notice of some other things
which may be said upon the animal and which they understand...

                              y.l.f.,[6]
                              T.B.

1] through his connections at Court, Edward Browne had acquired one of the
Moroccan ostriches   2] the waste-product of the brew-house   3] bran
sediments   4] preserved   5] the lecture-demonstration in an anatomy
theatre in which the subject is opened up by a surgeon   6] 'your loving father'

¶Notes on ostriches (to Edward Browne)

Feb. 5 [1681-2]
D.s.,
....I have enclosed these two heads of an ostrich which Frank suddenly drew out; figure 1 is the head as I find it in Bellonius, *De la Nature des Oiseaux*, in French, which book perhaps you cannot easily meet with; mine was printed at Paris, 1555. I doubt it will not well answer the head of yours. That of figure 2 is the head of one in Mr Willoughby's *Ornithologia*, and Mr Ray's, which many have; the heads are different; whether the head of a male and female be so different I know not, nor when authors set down the figures do they tell us whether they be of male or female, but such likely, as they had opportunity to see. The head in Willoughby's *Ornithologia* is different from that in Alrovandus or Johnstonus by that circular rising on the head. Look upon Mr Ray's cut in *Ornithologia*. Mark the foot well of yours, whether it hath any kind of teeth and the one division more horny than the other. The tail in all is round, not spread. You may read Ray's chapter on the ostrich; mine is in Latin. Nierembergius speaks of some ostriches to be found in America, but no[t] so well feathered as in Africa....
                           Y.l.f.
                           T.B.
[The ostrich died of cold in February; E. Browne dissected it and reported on it to T.B.]
                                                    Letters 207-08

¶More ostrich notes (to Edward Browne)

Feb 10, [1681-2]
D.S.,
I am glad you have done so much, if not in a manner all, in your ostrich business. The two papers you sent are very well done and with good exactness. I have read them often over [there follows a number of comments on Edward's dissection notes]....In your two papers sent there is enough to afford a large discourse, but things must be first writ briefly, whatever additions may be made hereafter; this being, I think, the first ostrich dissected in England, at least to my purpose.
                                                    Letters, 208-10

¶(to Edward Browne)

15 Feb [1681-2]
....Mr Clark tells me he saw two ostriches in London in Cromwell's
time. Though you saw an ostrich in the Duke of Florence's garden, yet
I do not perceive you saw any one among the curiosities and rarities of
any of the Princes of Germany. Perhaps the King will send some of his
to the King of France, the Prince of Orange, etc...

Letters 213

¶On the classification of animals
(to Christopher Merrett)

6 Feb [1668/9]
....I confess for such little birds I am much unsatisfied on the names
given to many by countrymen, and uncertain what to give them myself, or to what classis of authors clearly to reduce[1] them. Surely there
are many found among us which are not described, and therefore such
which you cannot well reduce may (if at all) be set down after the
exacter nomination of small birds, as yet of uncertain class or knowledge.
    I present you with a draught of a water fowl, not common, and
none of our fowlers can name it. The bill could not be exactly expressed by a coal or black chalk, whereby the little incurvity at the end
of the upper bill and small recurvity of the lower is not discerned. The
wings are very short, and it is fin-footed; the bill is strong and sharp. If
you name it not, I am uncertain what to call it; I may consider this
anatula,[2] or *mergulus melanoleucus rostro acuto*...[3]

Letters 356

¶Stork lore

....That storks are to be found and will only live in republics or free
states is a petty conceit to advance the opinion of popular policies, and
from antipathies in nature to disparage monarchical government. But
how far agreeable unto truth, let them consider who read in Pliny that

1]* what sort of book to find them in   2] the family of ducks   3] a black-
and-white sharp-billed duck, possibly the little pied cormorant

among the Thessalians who were governed by kings, and much
abounded with serpents, it was no less than capital[1] to kill a stork. That
the ancient Egyptians honoured them, whose government was from
all times monarchical, that Bellonius affirmeth men make them nests
in France, that relations make them common in Persia and the dominions of the great Turk, and lastly, how Jeremy the prophet delivered
himself to his countrymen, whose government was at that time
monarchical: 'The stork in the heaven knowing her appointed time,
the turtle, crane, and swallow observe the time of their coming, but
my people know not the judgement of the Lord.' Wherein to
exprobate[2] their stupidity, he induceth the providence of storks. Now
if the bird had been unknown, the illustration had been obscure, and
the exprobation not so proper....

PE III.xxvii. 256

A kind of stork was shot in the wing by the sea near Hasburrow and
brought alive unto me; it was about a yard high, red head, coloured
legs and bill, the claws resembling human nails, such as Herodotus
describeth in the white ibis of Egypt. The lower parts of the wings are
black, which gathered up makes the lower part of back look black, but
the tail under them is white as the other part of the body. It fed readily
upon snails and frogs, but a toad being offered, it would not touch it.
The tongue very short not an inch long. It makes a clattering noise by
flapping one bill against the other, somewhat like the *platea* or
shovelard.[3] The quills of the bigness of swan's bills. When it swallowed
a frog it was sent down into the stomach by the backside of the neck,
as was perceived upon swallowing. I could not but take notice of the
conceit of some who looked upon it as an ill omen, saying if storks
come over into England, pray God a commonwealth do not come
after.

Notes 415-16

¶Marine biology

Stellae marinae, or sea stars[1] in great plenty, especially about Yarmouth. Whether they be bred out of the *urticae*, squalders,[2] or sea
jellies, as many report, we cannot confirm, but the squalders in the

1] a capital offence   2] reproach them   3] spoonbill

1] star fishes   2] stinging jellyfish

middle seem to have some lines or first draughts not unlike. Our stars exceed not five points, though I have heard that some with more have been found about Hunstanton and Burnham, where are also found *stellae marinae testaceae*,[3] or handsome, crusted, and brittle sea stars, much less.

Notes 423

¶ Of corruption

....Some verity it may also have in itself, as truly declaring the corruptive constitution in the present sap and nutrimental juice of the tree, and may consequently discover the disposition[1] of that year according to the plenty or kinds of these productions. For if the putrefying juices of bodies bring forth plenty of flies and maggots, they give testimony of common corruption and declare that the elements are full of the seeds of putrefaction, as the great number of caterpillars, gnats, and ordinary insects do also declare. If they run into spiders, they give signs of higher putrefaction, as plenty of vipers and scorpions are confessed to do,[2] the putrefying materials producing animals of higher mischiefs according to the advance and higher strain of corruption....

PE II.vii.152

3] a shelled star fish or *ophiotrix fragilis*

1] the weather patterns   2] an unusual abundance of vermin were thought to signal an especially bad disposition of the elements in a given year

V. SIGNATURES

¶Figures in nature

Too much there is of obscurity in discovering the true intentions of figure,[1] and the prime end of nature therein, if we look not only upon mineral figurations,[2] but offer to assign a reason to the figures of leaves, flowers, and seeds, which notwithstanding specifically attend on plants and are not contrived in vain. Of better discovery are the artifices of birds and animals in their nests and places of habitation. How far nature geometrizeth[3] the beaver showeth in his nest and the spider in the web. Birds make their nest circular as the best for receptacle and capacity. No circles are more exact than such as are made by woodworms, and maggots in nuts....

Beside the outward and obvious figures and shapes of plants which obviously deliver their signatures, there are many hidden figures in the roots underground or inward parts above it, and these are generally made by the figure of the pores and conducts of the alimental juices and outward figure of the stalk which containeth them. Thus, the annual sprouts of the oak, being quinquangular upon incision, do make a figure which resembleth a star or five points, as in the stone *astroites*,[4] briar, the ash. The stalk of a fig makes a triangle, the incisions of young green walnuts as big as nuts leave notable white characters from the rudiments[5] of the half transversely cut.

The osmond, or water fern, being itself semicircular, cut near the root presents a rainbow or half the character of Pisces; the female fern a broad spread tree or spreadeackle,[6] wherein the root or feet arise always from the flat part and oppositely unto the lateral position of the leaves.

In carrots, parsnips and carnous roots appear flosculous figures,

1] signatures   2] figures found in stones   3]* works geometrically
4] star sapphire   5] the early and immature growth of the sapling
6] a tree with the shape of a spread eagle

and rosy expansions,[7] and in harder roots of *verbascum blattaria*[8] rosy figures with four or five points; in the common marsh sedge neat circles pointed like needlework, in which under the juice ascendeth unto the stalk.

Notes 246-8

¶Signatures

Studious observators may discover more analogies in the orderly book of nature, and cannot escape the elegancy of her hand in other correspondencies. The figures of nails and crucifying appurtenances are but precariously made out in the *Granadilla*[1] or flower of Christ's passion; and we despair to behold in these parts that handsome draught of crucifixion in the fruit of the Barbado pine.[2] The seminal spike of the *Phalaris*, or great shaking grass, more nearly answers the tail of a rattlesnake than many resemblances in Porta; and if the man-orchis of Columna[3] be well made out, it excelleth all analogies.[4] In young walnuts cut athwart it is not hard to apprehend strange charac-ters; and in those of somewhat elder growth, handsome ornamental draughts about a plain cross. In the root of osmond, or water fern, every eye may discern the form of a half moon, rainbow, or half the character of Pisces. Some find Hebrew, Arabic, Greek, and Latin char-acters in plants; in a common one among us we seem to read *Aiaia, Viviu, Lilil.*[5]

GC III.206-07

¶Physiognomy of virtue

....I have observed that those professed eleemosynaries,[1] though in a crowd or multitude, do yet direct and place their petitions on a few and selected persons. There is surely a physiognomy which those expe-

7] pink or red figures; or figures of roses   8] mullein

1] passionflower or *passiflora quadrangularis*   2] pineapple; but Browne really means the banana   3] a testicle-shaped plant described by Colonna   4] it is the best possible description of the plant   5] in the myth of Hyacinth, the beautiful boy beloved of Apollo, at his untimely death an iris-like flower arose from his blood which carries within its petals the mark αιαι, ('alas'). The other two signatures are obscure.

1] those who live upon alms

rienced and master-mendicants[2] observe, whereby they instantly discover a merciful aspect, and will single out a face wherein they spy the
signatures and marks of mercy. For there are mystically in our faces
certain characters which carry in them the motto of our souls, wherein
he that cannot read A.B.C. may read our natures. I hold, moreover,
that there is a phytognomy,[3] a physiognomy not only of men, but of
plants and vegetables; and in every one of them some outward figures
which hang as signs or bushes of their inward forms. The finger of God
hath set an inscription upon all his works, not graphical or composed
of letters, but of their several forms, constitutions, parts, and operations, which aptly joined together make one word that doth express
their natures. By these letters God calls the stars by their names, and by
this alphabet Adam assigned to every creature a name peculiar to its
nature. Now there are besides these characters in our faces, certain
mystical figures in our hands which I dare not call mere dashes,
strokes, *a la volée*, or at random, because delineated by a pencil that
never works in vain; and hereof I take more particular notice because
I carry that in mine own hand which I could never read of or discover
in another. Aristotle, I confess, in his acute and singular book of physiognomy,[4] hath made no mention of chiromancy;[5] yet I believe the
Egyptians, who were nearer addicted to those abstruse and mystical
sciences, had a knowledge therein, to which those vagabond and
counterfeit Egyptians[6] did after pretend, and perhaps retained a few
corrupted principles which sometimes might verify their
prognostics....

RM II.2

¶Of the hieroglyphical pictures of the Egyptians

Certainly of all men that suffered from the confusion of Babel, the
Egyptians found the best evasion, for though the words were confounded, they invented a language of things and spake unto each
other by common notions in nature. Whereby they discoursed in silence and were intuitively understood from the theory of their ex-
presses.[1] For they assumed the shapes of animals common unto all
eyes, and by their conjunctions and compositions were able to com-

2] master-beggars   3] the physiognomy of vegetables   4] *Physiognomica*
(once attributed to Aristotle)   5] palmistry   6] gypsies

1] hieroglyphics

municate their conceptions unto any that coapprehended the syntaxis of their natures.² This many conceive to have been the primitive way of writing, and of greater antiquity than letters; and this indeed might Adam well have spoken, who, understanding the nature of things, had the advantage of natural expressions;³ which the Egyptians but taking upon trust, upon their own or common opinion, from conceded mistakes they authentically promoted errors,⁴ describing in their hieroglyphics creatures of their own invention, or from known and conceded animals erecting significations not inferable from their natures.

And first, although there were more things in nature than words which did express them, yet even in these mute and silent discourses, to express complexed significations they took a liberty to compound and piece together creatures of allowable forms into mixtures inexistent. Thus began the descriptions of griffins, basilisks, phoenix, and many more, which emblematists and heralds have entertained with significations answering their institutions; hieroglyphically adding martegres, wyverns, lion-fishes,⁵ with divers others – pieces of good and allowable invention unto the prudent spectator, but are looked on by vulgar eyes as literal truths, or absurd impossibilities; whereas indeed, they are commendable inventions and of laudable significations....

A woman that hath but one child, they express by a lioness, for that conceiveth but once. Fecundity they set forth by a goat, because but seven days old it beginneth to use coition. The abortion of a woman they describe by an horse kicking a wolf, because a mare will cast her foal if she tread in the track of that animal. Deformity they signify by a bear;⁶ and an unstable man by an hyena, because that animal yearly exchangeth its sex. A woman delivered of a female child they imply by a bull looking over his left shoulder, because if in coition a bull part from a cow on that side the calf will prove a female.

All which, with many more, how far they consent with truth we

2] read the symbolical meanings assciated with various animals   3] Adam before the fall was able to name the animals because he was able to recognize their inherent names denoted by their outward forms   4] since the Egyptians did not have the advantage of this Adamic intuition about the meanings of things, they had to take as given certain misnomers, and thus errors about animals were perpetuated in their hieroglyphical system of writing   5] martegre or manticore, a mythical beast with a lion's body, man's head, porcupine quills, and a scorpion's tail; wyvern, a winged dragon with two eagle's feet and a serpent's tail; lionfish,** perhaps the scaly lion-shaped sea-monster   6] because bears bring forth their young in unformed lumps which only achieve their proper shapes by the mother's licking

shall not disparage our reader to dispute; and though some way allowable unto wiser conceits, who could distinctly receive their
significations, yet carrying the majesty of hieroglyphics, and so transmitted by authors, they crept into a belief with many, and favourable
doubt[7] with most. And thus, I fear, it hath fared with the hieroglyphical symbols of Scripture, which, excellently intended in the species of
things sacrificed, in the prohibited meats, in the dreams of Pharoah,
Joseph, and many other passages, are ofttimes wracked[8] beyond their
symbolisations, and enlarged into constructions disparaging their true
intentions.

PE V.xx.379-81

¶Of earthly beauty[1]

....Cupid is said to be blind; affection should not be too sharp-sighted,
and love not to be made by magnifying glasses. If things were seen as
they are, the beauty of bodies would be much abridged; and therefore
the wisdom of God hath drawn the pictures and outsides of things
softly and amiably unto the natural edge of our eyes, not able to discover those unlovely asperities which make oystershells in good faces,
and hedgehogs even in Venus moles[2]....

CP 288

....That Augustus had native notes on his body and belly after the
order and number in the stars of Charles' Wain[3] will not seem strange
unto astral physiognomy,[4] which accordingly considereth moles in the
body of man; or physical observators, who from the position of moles
in the face reduce them to rule and correspondency in other parts.[5]
Whether after the like method medical conjecture may not be raised
upon parts inwardly affected – since parts about the lips are the critical
seats of pustules discharged in agues, and scrofulous tumours about
the neck do so often speak the like about the mesentery[6] – may also be
considered....

GC III.207-08

7] doubt tempered by a disposition to believe   8] stretched, deformed

1] see *CM*, p.265 [p. 00]   2] beauty spots   3] the constellation Ursa Major
4] the likeness of marks on the body to constellations   5] make the pattern of
facial moles correspond to physical patterns and dispositions of other parts of the
body   6] an eruption of the skin which (in early medicine) signalled a similar
disease of the intestinal tissue

¶ Of the quincunx

....Now the number of five is remarkable in every circle, not only as the first spherical number,[1] but the measure of spherical motion. For spherical bodies move by fives, and every globular figure placed upon a plane, in direct volutation,[2] returns to the first point of contaction in the fifth touch,[3] accounting by the axes of the diameters or cardinal points of the four quarters thereof. And before it arriveth unto the same point again, it maketh five circles equal unto itself, in each progress from those quarters absolving an equal circle.[4]

By the same number doth nature divide the circle of the sea-star, and in that order and number disposeth those elegant semicircles, or dental sockets and eggs, in the sea hedgehog.[5] And no mean observations hereof there is in mathematics of the nearest retiary[6] spider, which concluding in forty-four circles, from five semidiameters beginneth that elegant texture.[7]

And after this manner doth lay the foundation of the circular branches of the oak, which being five-cornered in the tender annual sprouts, and manifesting upon incision the signature of a star, is after made circular and swelled into a round body; which practice of nature is become a point of art, and makes two problems in Euclid.[8] But the bramble which sends forth shoots and prickles from its angles maintains its pentagonal figure and the unobserved signature of a handsome porch within it (to omit the five small buttons dividing the circle of the ivy-berry, and the five characters in the winter stalk of the walnut, with many other observables which cannot escape the eyes of signal discerners, such as know where to find Ajax his name in delphinium, or Aaron's mitre in henbane).[9]

Quincuncial forms and ordinations are also observable in animal figurations. For to omit the *hyoides* or throat-bone of animals; the *furcula* or merry-thought[10] in birds, which supporteth the *scapulae*, affording a passage for the windpipe and the gullet; the wings of flies, and disposure of their legs in their first formation from maggots, and the position of their horns, wings, and legs in their aurelian cases[11] and

1] the first whole number (not counting one) which squared yields a figure whose last digit is itself   2] rolling   3] place at which a rolling object comes to rest
4] when a sphere is rolled upon a flat surface it will have covered five times its own area by the time it reaches its starting point again   5] sea-urchin   6] web-making   7] makes the web with five spokes or threads radiating from the centre and forty-four circular threads   8] in his *Elements*   9] examples of so-called signatures in plants   10] breastbone   11] chrysales

swaddling clouts; the back of the *cimex arboreus*,[12] found often upon trees and lesser plants, doth elegantly discover the Burgundian decussation;[13] and the like is observable in the belly of the *Notonecton*, or water-beetle, which swimmeth on its back, and the handsome rhombusses of the sea-poult, or weasel,[14] on either side of the spine.

GC III.201-02

¶ More quincunxes

Physicians are not without the use of this decussation[1] in several operations, in ligatures and union of dissolved continuities.[2] Mechanics[3] make use hereof in forcipal organs,[4] and instruments of incision, wherein who can but magnify the power of decussation, inservient[5] to contrary ends: solution and consolidation, union, and divisions; illustrable from Aristotle in the old *Nucifragium* or nutcracker, and the instruments of evulsion,[6] compression or incision, which consisting of two *vectes* or arms converted towards each other, the innitency[7] and stress being made upon the *hypomochlion* or fulciment[8] in the decussation, the greater compression is made by the union of two impulsors....

The same[9] is not forgot by lapidaries while they cut their gems pyramidally, or by equicural[10] triangles. Perspective picturers,[11] in their base, horizon, and lines of distances, cannot escape these rhomboidal decussations. Sculptors,[12] in their strongest shadows, after this order do draw their double hatches. And the very Americans[13] do naturally fall upon it in their neat and curious textures, which is also observed in the elegant artifices of Europe. But this is no law unto the woof of the neat retiary spider, which seems to weave without transversion,[14] and by the union of right lines to make out a continued surface which is beyond the common art of textury, and may still nettle

---

12] the capsid bug   13] rays or lines crossed to form a rhomboid X shape; here a saltire, or St Andrew's cross   14] the *mustela* or rockling fish

---

1] see n.13 above   2] in the binding up of severed arteries and of other separated or damaged parts of the body   3] artisans   4] forceps   5] assisting
6] pulling out by force   7] pressure   8] fulcrum   9] the quincuncial pattern   10] isosceles   11] painters who use the laws of perspective
12] engravers   13] American indians   14] turning across or athwart; the spider spins its web only in straight lines, yet produces a pattern of many angles

Minerva, the goddess of that mystery.[15] And he that shall hatch the little seeds, either found in small webs, or white round eggs carried under the bellies of some spiders, and behold how at their first production[16] in boxes they will presently fill the same with their webs, may observe the early and untaught finger of nature and how they are natively provided with a stock sufficient for such texture....

GC II.188-9

¶Signatures and adumbration

...But seeds themselves do lie in perpetual shades, either under the leaf, or shut up in coverings; and such as lie barest have their husks, skins, and pulps about them, wherein the neb and generative particle lieth moist and secured from the injury of air and sun. Darkness and light hold interchangeable dominions, and alternately rule the seminal state of things. Light unto Pluto is darkness unto Jupiter. Legions of seminal ideas lie in their second chaos and Orcus of Hippocrates,[1] till putting on the habits of their forms, they show themselves upon the stage of the world and open dominion of Jove. They that held the stars of heaven were but rays and flashing glimpses of the empyreal light through holes and perforations of the upper heaven[2] took off the natural shadows of stars,[3] while according to better dicovery the poor inhabitants of the moon have but a polary[4] life, and must pass half their days in the shadow of that luminary.

Light that makes things seen, makes some things invisible. Were it nor for darkness and the shadow of the earth the noblest part of the creation had remained unseen, and the stars in heaven as invisible as on the fourth day, when they were created above the horizon with the sun, or there was not an eye to behold them. The greatest mystery of religion is expressed by adumbration,[5] and in the noblest part of Jewish types we find the cherubims shadowing the mercy-seat.[6] Life itself

15] Minerva and Arachne competed as weavers; Arachne was turned into a spider by the goddess, who could find no fault with her work   16] after hatching

1] Hippocrates imagined that darkness is a kind of light in the underworld (Orcus, ruled by Pluto), but that the light of the upper world (ruled by Jupiter) is a shadow there   2] so Hevelius, *Selenographia* (1647)   3] denied eclipses and occultations of heavenly bodies   4] polarized   5] symbolically; in outline; by shadowed representation   6] 'cherubims of glory shadowing the mercy-seat' (the golden covering on the Ark of the Covenant) (Hebrews 9:5), were types of Christ's incarnation ('the power of the Highest shall overshadow thee' (Luke 1:35))

is but the shadow of death, and souls departed but the shadows of the living. All things fall under this name.[7] The sun itself is but the dark simulacrum,[8] and light but the shadow of God.[9]

GC IV.218

7] everything may be described as a shadow of a higher principle   8] a shadowy representation   9] a translation of Ficino's well-known Neoplatonic remark *Lux est umbra dei*, quoted rather more impatiently by Browne in *RM* I.10

VI. MEDICINE

¶ Venereal disease (to Edward Browne)

May 17 [1679]
D. s.,
....You will, I hope, receive a letter from me by Mr Augustine Blennerhasett of this country, who goeth toward London on Monday; he was with you in London a year or two ago and hath a good respect for you. He saith he had the gonorrhoea some years past which came but at times; at Michaelmas last he complained of some pain in the genitals and swelling and gleeting,[1] as he called it, at the penis, and lying at his house at the Lathes by Pockthorp gates consulted Dr Blincolne whom he knew, and afterward both of us prescribed many medicines, and he took mercurial pills for some time, but they did not raise a salivation or very little;[2] drinks also of sarsa and guaiac. etc.;[3] and when not mercurial,[4] then he took since for a good while pills of rhubarb cum gum guiac., terebinth.[5] etc; so he said he was pretty well and rode about and took nothing more, and I saw him again but lately, he being as I think subpoenaed up to London. I wished him to come unto you and have the part examined well, which I have seen but once or twice, and so you may call in my cousin Hobbes, and may diligently consider two things, that is, whether he hath any remainder of the gonorrhoea, and also what causeth a weakness in the erection, which he was first sensible of upon overstraining with a woman, as he saith, which are materially to be considered, he having an intention to marry, and hath settled his affection upon a gentlewoman, and these are material points in reference unto them both. Give him between you the best satisfaction without great discouragement, yet with truth.

1] discharging of thin, purulent matter   2] the administration of mercury to effect excess salivation was a standard practice in the treatment of venereal diseases
3] taken for venereal complaints   4] taking mercury pills (a venereal remedy)
5] turpentine

He is hypochondriacal, meticulous and diffident, and apt to lay hold of what you say. If anything will be attempted effectual to his relief, he will stay three weeks, if not a month, to attend it, and he had better do so than to ride about and do little for himself and have his thoughts only possessed with marrying; but this you need not take notice of but from himself when you ask whether he intendeth marriage or in how long time; do all with best secrecy, for that will give him best content. He is a kind gentleman and not intemperate, at least not of late; he was eldest son unto Mr Hasset, and his father hath been dead many years....

Y.l.f.

T. Browne

I doubt the R. Society doth little now; we have not heard much of it of late.

Letters 107-08

¶ Medical gossip (to Edward Browne)

Nov 11, [1680]

D.s.

I have perused D.C.'s oration[1] which is good, but long; where it was delivered, either in the hall of the college or anatomy theatre,[2] I know not, but, however, Cutler being one of the benefactors and founder of the theatre, something may be said not only of his commendation, but of the theatre itself; not only of the largeness, stateliness, & noble contrivance, but also comparatively to other outlandish theatres which you have seen, as of Vienna, Altdorf, Leyden, Padua, Montpellier, and Paris, for I know not whether you took notice of Pisa, Rome, and any other whereof you may advertise me if you observed anything about them....

I writ to you lately of the poor woman of an hundred and five years old lacking one month; she hath had this continual autumnal tertian fever,[3] and there is good hopes of her recovery, for she can now rise and set up out of her bed, and desires a little wine which she could [not] endure in her distemper. Your sisters saw her yesterday who used to give her money. She sees so well that she knew them at a distance

---

1] Dr Walter Charlton, who gave the Harveian Oration in 1680 to the Royal College of Physicians   2] the Cutlerian Anatomical Theatre of the Royal College of Physicians   3] a malarial fever whose acute symptoms recur every three days

and her hearing is good. Formerly they gave not the cortex[4] to quartanarians[5] before they had been ill a considerable time, but I think it should be good to give it at the beginning before their bloods are corrupted by the length of the disease. Write whe[ther] they do not give it early in London.

Y.l.f.

T.B.

Letters 169-70

¶ Laterality in medicine

....what admission[1] we owe unto many conceptions concerning right and left requireth circumspection. That is, how far we ought to rely upon the remedy of Kiranides – that is, the left eye of an hedgehog fried in oil to procure sleep, and the right foot of a frog in a deer's skin for the gout; or that to dream of the loss of right or left tooth presageth the death of male or female kindred according to the doctrine of Artemidorus; what verity there is in that numeral conceit[2] in the lateral division of man by even and odd, ascribing the odd unto the right side, and even unto the left, and so by parity or imparity of letters in men's names to determined misfortunes on either side of their bodies (by which account in Greek numeration, Hephaestus or Vulcan was lame in the right foot, and Hannibal lost his right eye; and lastly, what substance there is in that auspicial[3] principle and fundamental doctrine of ariolation[4] that the left hand is ominous[5] and that good things do pass sinistrously[6] upon us because the left hand of man respected the right hand of the gods, which handed their favours unto us.

PE IV.v.286-7

4]* a medicine made from the bark of various trees
5] those suffering from episodic malarial agues which recur every four days

1] acknowledgement or concession   2] the Pythagorean belief that by calculating the numerical value of the letters of the name divinations could be made of illness or disability on particular sides of the body   3]* oracular
4]* soothsaying   5] lucky, of good omen   6] from the left

VII. ADVICE

¶Tourist advice (to young Thomas Browne)

Dec 22 [1660]
Honest Tom,
I hope by God's assistance you have been some weeks in Bordeaux. I
was yesterday at Yarmouth, where I spoke with your uncle Charles
Mileham, who told me Mr Dade[1] would accommodate you with what
moneys were fitting for defray of your charges in any kind, and therefore would not have me at present send you any bill to receive any
particular sum; but however when I hear from you I will take care for
such a bill to be sent to Mr Dade, to whom in the mean time present
my true respects and service and be sure to be observant of what he
shall advise you; be as good a husband[2] as possible and enter not upon
any course of superfluous expenses; be not dejected and melancholy
because you can yet have little comfort in conversation, and all things
will seem strange unto you. Remember the camel's back[3] and be not
troubled for anything that other ways would trouble your patience
here, be courteous and civil to all, put on a decent boldness and avoid
pudor rusticus,[4] not much known in France; hold firm to the Protestant religion and be diligent in going to church when you have any
little knowledge of the language. God will accept of your desires to
serve him in his public worship, though you cannot make it out to
your desires;[5] be constant, not negligent, in your daily private prayers
and habituate your heart in your tender days unto the fear and reverence of God. It were good you had a map of France that you might not
be unacquainted with the several parts and to resort unto upon occasion for your information; view and understand all notable buildings
and places in Bordeaux or near it, and take a draught thereof, as also
the ruined amphitheatre, but these at your leisure; there is, I think, a

1] a friend of the family living in Bordeaux   2] manager of personal affairs
3] perhaps 'do not try to do everything at once.'   4] shyness and lack of sophis-
tication   5] you cannot understand it as well as you would like

book in French called *Le[s] Monuments* or *Les Antiquites de Bordeaux*;
enquire of the same; read some books of French or Latin, for I would
by no means you should lose your Latin but rather gain more.

Ned⁶ comes not home this Xtmas. I shall, God willing, remember
your New Year's gift; give me an account of your voyage by sea as
particular as you can, for I doubt⁷ you had a rough passage; be temperate in diet and wary to overheat your self; remember to *comprimere et
non extendere labra*;⁸ to God's providence I commit you.

Vostre tres chere Pere,
Tho Browne

I have sent a little box by this ship.

Letters 3-4

¶Financial prudence (to Edward Browne)

Aug 22 [1680]
D.S.,
I was very glad to receive your last letter. God hath heard our prayers
and I hope will bless you still. If the profits of the next year come not
up to this I would not have you discouraged, for the profits of no
practice are equal or regular, and you have had some extraordinary
patients¹ this year, which perhaps some years will not afford. Now is
your time to be frugal and lay up. I thought myself rich enough till my
children grew up.² Be careful of yourself and temperate, that you may
be able to go through your practice; for to attain to the getting of a
thousand pounds a year requires no small labour of body and mind,
and is a life not much less painful and laborious than that which the
meaner sort of people go through. When you put out your money be
well assured of the assurance,³ and be wise therein from what your
father hath suffered.⁴ It is laudable to dwell handsomely, but be not
too forward to build or set forth another man's house, or so to fill it

---

6] Edward Browne, then at Trinity College, Cambridge   7] do not
doubt   8] 'to close, not open, your lips' (i.e. don't talk too much)

1] possibly Charles II and other powerful persons at Court   2] Browne wrote
on another occasion to Edward: 'The christenings and burials of my children have
cost me about two hundred pounds, and their education more; beside your own,
which hath been more than all the rest put together.'   3] be certain of the
guarantee (or of the security given in exchange)   4] Browne had had various
financial difficulties in the course of a long life and a large family

that it may increase the fuel, if God should please to send fire. The merciful God direct you in all.

Excess in apparel and chargeable[5] dresses are got into the country, especially among women; men go decently and plain enough. The last Assizes[6] there was a concourse of women at that they call my Lord's garden in Cunsford, and so richly dressed that some strangers said there was scarce the like to be seen at Hyde Park, which makes charity cold. We now hear that this parliament shall sit the 21st of October, which will make London very full in Michaelmas Term. We hear of two ostriches which are brought from Tangier. I doubt these will not be shown at Bartholomew Fair[7] where everyone may see them for his money. I have read all or most of Dr Love's book,[8] which is a pretty good book and gives a good account of the Low Country practice in that disease and hath some other observables. I knew one Mr Christopher Love, son unto Dr Love, Warden of Winchester College, who was an active man against the King in the late wars and got a great estate, but I think he was fain to fly upon the King's restoration...God bless my daughter Browne and you all.

Y.l.f.
T.B.

Letters 156-7

¶ Of charity

'Give not only unto seven, but also unto eight',[1] that is, unto more than many. Though to 'give unto every one that asketh',[2] may seem severe advice, yet give thou also before asking, that is, where want is silently clamorous, and men's necessities, not their tongues, do loudly call for thy mercies. For though sometimes necessitousness be dumb, or misery speak not out, yet true charity is sagacious and will find out hints for beneficence. Acquaint thyself with the physiognomy of want, and let the dead colours and first lines of necessity suffice to tell thee there is an object for thy bounty. Spare not where thou canst not easily be prodigal, and fear not to be undone by mercy. For since 'he who hath pity on the poor lendeth unto the Almighty Rewarder',[3] who

---

5] expensive   6] periodic session of local courts for civil and criminal cases   7] annual trade and amusement fair held in Smithfield in London in late August   8] *De Morbo Epidemico* (1679)

1] Ecclesiasticus 11:2   2] Luke 6:30   3] Proverbs 19:17

observes no ides[4] but every day for his payments, charity becomes pious usury, Christian liberality the most thriving industry, and what we adventure in a cockboat[5] may return in a carrack[6] unto us. He who thus casts his bread upon the water shall surely find it again;[7] for though it falleth to the bottom, it sinks but like the axe of the prophet,[8] to arise again unto him.

CM I.6

¶ *Nosce teipsum*

Behold thyself by inward optics and the crystalline[1] of thy soul. Strange it is that in the most perfect sense there should be so many fallacies that we are fain to make a doctrine, and often to see by art;[2] but the greatest imperfection is in our inward sight, that is, to be ghosts unto our own eyes, and while we are so sharp-sighted as to look through others, to be invisible to ourselves; for the inward eyes are more fallacious than the outward. The vices we scoff at in others laugh at us within ourselves. Avarice, pride, falsehood lie undiscerned and blindly in us, even to the age of blindness: and therefore to see ourselves interiorly we are fain to borrow other men's eyes, wherein true friends are good informers, and censurers no bad friends. Conscience only, that can see without light, sits in the areopagy[3] and dark tribunal of our hearts, surveying our thoughts and condemning their obliquities... In the city of the new Jerusalem[4] there is neither sun nor moon, where glorified eyes must see by the archetypal sun,[5] or the light of God, able to illuminate intellectual eyes[6] and make unknown visions. Intuitive perceptions in spiritual beings may perhaps hold some analogy unto vision, but yet how they see us, or one another, what eye, what light, or what perception is required unto their intuition, is yet dark unto our apprehension; and even how they see God,

4] the 15th or the 13th of each month in the Roman calendar   5] a small boat   6] a large warship   7] Ecclesiastes 11:1   8] in Jordan, where the sons of Elishah went to build their houses, an axe-head which fell in the water was retrieved by casting a stick after it, which made it rise to the surface (2 Kings 6:4-6)

1] the lenses of the eyes   2] it is bad enough that our misunderstandings of the world prompt us to explain it by theories   3] a secret tribunal   4] foretold in Revelation 21:2, the city founded by God for the just after the Apocalypse   5] ideally present in its original or primitive form to the divine mind and to the human intellect (rather than to the senses)   6] i.e. not apprehensible by the senses

or how unto our glorified eyes the beatifical vision will be celebrated,
another world must tell us, when perceptions will be new and we may
hope to behold invisibles.

CM III.15

¶ Sincerity

Though the world be histrionical,[1] and most men live ironically, yet be
thou what thou singly art and personate only thyself. Swim smoothly
in the stream of thy nature, and live but one man. To single hearts
doubling is discruciating;[2] such tempers must sweat to dissemble, and
prove but hypocritical hypocrites. Simulation must be short: men do
not easily continue a counterfeiting life or dissemble unto death. He
who counterfeiteth acts a part, and is as it were out of himself, which,
if long, proves so irksome that men are glad to pull off their vizards,[3]
and resume themselves again; no practice being able to naturalise such
unnaturals, or make a man rest content not to be himself. And therefore, since sincerity is thy temper, let veracity be thy virtue in words,
manners and actions. To offer at iniquities which have so little foundations in thee were to be vicious uphill and strain for thy condemnation.
Persons viciously inclined want no wheels to make them actively vicious, as having the elater and spring[4] of their own natures to facilitate
their iniquities. And therefore so many who are sinistrous[5] unto good
actions are ambidexterous unto bad, and Vulcans in virtuous paths,
Achilleses in vicious motions.[6]

CM III.20

¶ Humility

Be substantially great in thyself and more than thou appearest unto
others; and let the world be deceived in thee as they are in the lights of
heaven. Hang early plummets[1] upon the heels of pride, and let ambition have but an epicycle[2] or narrow circuit in thee. Measure not

1] acting a part; hypocritical   2] tormenting   3] masks; false fronts
4] expansiveness and elasticity   5] malign, corrupt, prejudiced   6] Vulcan
was lame; Achilles, by contrast, was a great warrior

1] mason's plumb-lines; figuratively, weights hung in order to impede motion
2] from Ptolemaic astronomy, one of the successive small circles which together
described the large circles of planetary orbits through the heavens

thyself by thy morning shadow[3] but by the extent of thy grave; and reckon thyself above the earth by the line[4] thou must be contented with under it. Spread not into boundless expansions either of designs or desires. Think not that mankind liveth but for a few, and that the rest are born but to serve the ambition of those who make but flies of men, and wildernesses of whole nations. Swell not into actions which embroil and confound the earth; but be one of those violent ones which force the kingdom of heaven.[5] If thou must needs reign, be Zeno's king,[6] and enjoy that empire[7] which every man gives himself. Certainly the iterated injunctions of Christ unto humility, meekness, patience, and that despised train of virtues cannot but make pathetical impressions upon those who have well considered the affairs of all ages, wherein pride, ambition, and vainglory have led up the worst of actions, and whereunto confusion, tragedies, and acts denying all religion do owe their originals.

Rest not in an ovation,[8] but a triumph over thy passions; chain up the unruly legion of thy breast;[9] behold thy trophies within thee, not without thee; lead thine own captivity captive, and be Caesar unto thyself.

Give no quarter unto those vices which are of thine inward family and, having a root in thy temper, plead a right and propriety in thee. Examine well thy complexional inclinations. Raise early batteries[10] against those strongholds built upon the rock of nature,[11] and make this a great part of the militia of thy life. The politic nature of vice must be opposed by policy,[12] and therefore wiser honesties project and plot against sin; wherein notwithstanding we are not to rest in generals, or the trite stratagems of art.[13] That may succeed with one temper which may prove successless with another. There is no community or commonwealth of virtue; every man must study his own œconomy[14] and erect these rules unto the figure of himself.

3] i.e. when shadows are long; figuratively, when you are in your prime
4] the length of a grave   5] struggle to enter the kingdom of heaven (Matthew 11:12)   6] the ideal wise man and ruler imagined by Zeno the Stoic philosopher; Cicero paraphrases the concept of the wise man as more kingly than Tarquin, more masterful than Sulla, and richer than Crassus, since, with moral worth the only true good and thing of value, the wise man owns all, and, not valuing the world, is truly free of all worldly constraint (Cicero, *De Finibus* III.22)
7] virtue   8] 'a petty and minor kind of triumph'   9] Legion was the collective name of all the demons which possessed the man of unclean spirit (Mark 5:9)
10] attacks   11] worldly vices to which mankind is constitutionally prone
12] the canny nature of vice to promote itself must be countered by equal sagacity and shrewdness   13] we must each tailor our defences against sin to our own needs rather than rely on generally advocated remedies   14] figuratively, good spiritual housekeeping

Lastly, if length of days be thy portion, make it not thy expectation; reckon not upon long life but live always beyond thy account. He that so often surviveth his expectation lives many lives and will hardly complain of the shortness of his days. Time past is gone like a shadow; make times to come, present; conceive that near which may be far off; approximate thy last times by present apprehensions of them; live like a neighbour unto death and think there is but little to come. And since there is something in us that must still live on, join both lives together; unite them in thy thoughts and actions and live in one but for the other. He who thus ordereth the purposes of this life will never be far from the next, and is in some manner already in it by an happy conformity and close apprehension of it.

LF 117

¶ L'envoi

But the quincunx of heaven[1] runs low, and 'tis time to close the five ports of knowledge.[2] We are unwilling to spin out our awaking thoughts into the phantasms of sleep, which too often continueth precogitations,[3] making cables of cobwebs and wildernesses of handsome groves. Beside, Hippocrates hath spoke so little,[4] and the oneirocritical masters[5] have left such frigid interpretations from plants, that there is little encouragement to dream of paradise itself. Nor will the sweetest delight of gardens afford much comfort in sleep, wherein the dullness of that sense shakes hands with delectable odours, and though in the bed of Cleopatra,[6] can hardly with any delight raise up the ghost of a rose.

Night, which pagan theology could make the daughter of Chaos, affords no advantage to the description of order, although no lower than that mass[7] can we derive its genealogy. All things began in order; so shall they end; and so shall they begin again, according to the ordainer of order and mystical mathematics of the city of heaven.

Though Somnus in Homer be sent to rouse up Agamemnon,[8] I find no such effects in the drowsy approaches of sleep. To keep our eyes open longer were but to act our antipodes.[9] The huntsmen are up in America, and they are already past their first sleep in Persia. But who can be drowsy at that hour which freed us from everlasting sleep,[10] or have slumbering thoughts at that time when sleep itself must end, and, as some conjecture, all shall awake again?[11]

GC V.225-6

FINIS

1] the Hyades   2] the five senses   3] earlier thoughts   4] credited with a work on dreams   5] those who interpret dreams, especially the Greek Artemidorus and the Arab Apomazar   6] her bed was said to have been covered with roses   7] nothing existed before Chaos   8] Zeus sent a false dream to Agamemnon, the king of Argos, encouraging him to attack Troy   9] to act as if it were day, as it would be on the other side of the world   10] Browne perhaps refers to the moment of Christ's resurrection, traditionally held to have occurred before dawn, which freed man from eternal death; or perhaps more generally to the notion that sleep is a preview of death, and that to fall asleep is like dying   11] the general resurrection of the dead at the Last Judgement

LIST OF PROPER NAMES

Achilles: Greek hero at Troy
Adrian: Hadrian or Adrianus, 2nd c. Roman emperor
Aelian: 3rd c. Roman historian
Agamemnon: the king of Argos and leader of the Greeks at Troy
Ajax Oileus: the 'lesser' Ajax of Homer, a warrior hated and destroyed
    by the gods
Ajax Telamonius: boastful and arrogant Greek hero at Troy
Alaricus: 4th-5th c. Visigothic conqueror of Rome
Albertus Magnus: 13th c. saint and Scholastic philosopher
Aldrovandus: 16th c. Italian naturalist
Ambrose: 4th c. saint, theologian and bishop of Milan
Amphilocus: a mythological participant in the Trojan War who, with
    Mopsus, later shared an oracle shrine at Cilicia in Asia Minor
Andreas: 3rd c. BC Egyptian medic
Angelo: Michaelangelo
Antonini: the Roman emperors who took the surname Antoninus
    (late 1st to late 2nd c.)
Antony: (Antony Abbot, or Antony of the Desert) 3rd-4th c. Egyp-
    tian saint who lived in a tomb in the desert as a hermit and was
    tormented by Satan with lewd and horrible visions
Apicius: 1st c. Roman cookery writer whom Browne translated
Apollo Daphnaeus: a prophetess
Apuleius: 2nd c. Greek Platonic philosopher and author of *The Golden*
    Ass
Archelaus: 5th c. BC Greek natural historian
Archemorus: Theban infant whose funeral pyre is described by
    Statius
Archimedes: 3rd c. BC Greek mathematician and inventor
Aretinus, Petrus: Pietro Aretino, 16th c. poet, dramatist, and satirist,
    soi-disant 'scourge of princes', who was most famous in his own
    time for scurrilous and insolent attacks upon the powerful

Aristotle: 4th c. BC Greek philosopher and scientist whose work, supremely influential in western and Islamic thought, was the foundation of medieval and Renaissance science and philosophy
Artemidorus: late 2nd-early 3rd c. Greek writer on the interpretation of dreams
Athanasius: 3rd-4th c. theologian of the eastern Church
Atropos: or Morta, one of the three Fates in Greek mythology; Atropos cut the thread of life
Augustus: the first Roman emperor (1st c.)
Austin: St Augustine, 4th-5th c. Bishop of Hippo, theologian, and one of the Fathers of the Church
Avicenna: 10th-11th c. Persian Aristotelian philosopher, scientist, and medic

Bacchus: or Dionysus, god of an ecstatic religious cult centred in Thrace
Barcephas: Moses Bar-Cepha, a 9th-10th century Syrian Biblical scholar
Beda: (Bede) 7th-8th c. English monk and historian of England
Bellini: 17th c. Italian anatomist
Bellonius: 16th c. French medic and naturalist
Berosus: 3rd c. BC Babylonian historian
Bosio: 16th-17th c. Italian archaeologist
Brassavolus: 16th c. Italian medical writer
Brennus: 4th c. BC Gallic king
Britannicus: son of the emperor Claudius; prevented from becoming emperor by the preferment of Nero
Brocardus: 15th c. Italian/Swiss writer on the Holy Land
Browne, Edward: (1642-1708) Browne's eldest son, also a doctor; physician to Charles II, Fellow of Royal Society, President of the Royal College of Physicians
Browne, Thomas: Browne's second son, 'Honest Tom' (1646-1667) was adventurous and intellectually gifted. A lieutenant in the navy, he probably died at sea, possibly in action

Cabeus: 16th-17th c. Italian mathematician
Cadmus: the legendary founder of Thebes, (married to Harmony)
Caesar, Julius: Roman triumvir and historian
Caligula: decadent 1st c. Roman emperor, assassinated in AD 41
Cambyses: 6th c. BC king of Persia who conquered Egypt
Camden, William: 16th-17th c. English antiquarian and schoolmaster

Canute: 11th c. king of England and Denmark

Caracalla: 3rd c. Roman emperor

Cardan: 16th c. Italian mathematician, astrologer, and medic
Casalius: 17th c. Italian antiquary

Casaubon, Meric: 17th c. English polymath, Biblical and classical scholar and translator, and investigator of spirits. He accused Dee of fraudulence

Cassiodorus: 5th-6th c. Roman monk

Cassius: one of Caligula's assassins (in AD 41)

Cato: 1st c. BC Roman tribune, Stoic philosopher, and opponent of Caesar

Cedrenus: 11th c. historian of the world

Charles V: (1500-58), Holy Roman Emperor, King of Spain, and Archduke of Austria; thus inheritor of the Hapsburg and Spanish empires; a major European power in the first half of the 16th c.

Charlton, Walter: sometime physician to Charles I and II, and President of the Royal College of Physicians

Cheops: 3rd millenium BC king of Egypt

Cheremon of Alexandria: 4th c. BC Greek hieroglyphical writer

Childeric: 5th c. Frankish king

Claudius: 1st c. Roman emperor

Clusius: 16th c. Dutch medic and botanist

Clytemnestra: wife and murderer of Agamemnon

Codignus: Nicolao Godinho, 17th c. Portugese travel writer

Columella: 1st c. Roman authority on agriculture and trees

Columnus/Colonna: 16th-17th c. Italian naturalist

Commodus: 2nd c. Roman emperor

Constans: 4th c. Roman emperor

Constantine: 4th c. Roman emperor primarily responsible for legitimizing Christianity within the Roman empire

Copernicus: 15th-16th c. Polish astronomer and theorist of heliocentrism

Cornelius Sylla: 2nd c. BC Roman general

Cotton, Sir Robert: 16th-17th c. English baronet and antiquary whose collection of manuscripts form an important part of the holdings of the British Library

Croesus: 6th c. BC Lydian king of fabulous wealth

Cuthred: 8th c. ruler of the West Saxons

Cutler, Sir John: wealthy London merchant who built the anatomy theatre for the Royal College of Physicians in 1678/9

Dante: Dante Alighieri, 13th-14th c. Florentine poet, author of the Christian epic *The Divine Comedy* and of *La Vita Nuova*

Dee, John: 16th c. English astrologer, chemist, and mathematician who found favour in the Elizabethan court and in the Imperial court at Prague

Della Porta: 16th-17th c. Italian naturalist and signaturist

Demetrius: one of several speakers in Plutarch's *De Defectu Oraculorum* (On the obsolescence of oracles)

Democritus: 5th-4th c. BC Greek philosopher and mocker of human foibles

Demosthenes: 4th c. BC Athenian orator

Dio[n] Cassius: 2nd-3rd c. Roman historian of the last years of the republic and of the early empire

Diocletian: 3rd-4th c. Roman emperor

Diodorus: 1st c. BC Greek historian

Dioscorides: 1st c. BC Greek medical writer

Domitian: 1st c. Roman emperor

Dugdale, Sir William: 17th c. English historian and antiquarian

Empedocles: 5th c. BC Sicilian Greek philosopher, poet, physiologist

Epicurus: 4th-3rd c. BC Greek ethical philosopher, founder of the Epicurean school

Epius: Hellenistic hieroglyphical writer

Estius: 16th-17th c. French Biblical scholar

Eucherius: 5th c. French bishop and theologian

Euclid: 4th c. BC Greek mathematician

Eugubinus: 16th c. theologian

Eusebius: 3rd-4th c. Palestinian theologian, Christian historian and biographer of Emperor Constantine

Eustathius: 12th c. Greek commentator on Homer

Fagius: 16th c. Hebraicist, theologian, and Biblical commentator

Frotho the Great: legendary Danish king

Galen: 2nd c. Greek physician, founder of experimental physiology

Gallienus: 3rd c. Roman emperor

Gassendus: 17th c. French mathematician and medic

Gemistus: 14th-15th c. Byzantine neoplatonic philosopher

Gesner: 16th c. Swiss naturalist

Germanicus: *see* Caligula

Geta: 3rd c. Roman emperor

Gordianus: 3rd c. Roman emperor

Goropius Becanus: 16th-17th c. Jesuit theologian of Brabant

Gregorius Turonensis: Gregory of Tours, 6th c. French saint, bishop, and historian

Grotius: 16th-17th c. Dutch legal scholar

Gruter: 16th-17th c. Dutch antiquarian and author of *Ancient Inscriptions* (1602-03)

Gulielmus: William of Paris, 12th-13th c. French philosopher- theologian

Hannibal: Carthaginian general who fought against Rome in the Second Punic War (218-201 BC)

Harald: 8th c. King of the Danes; killed by Ringo

Hector: Trojan hero and son of King Priam, killed at Troy

Helena: saint and mother of Emperor Constantine; claimed to have discovered pieces of the True Cross

Heliogabalus: 3rd c. Roman emperor

Heraclitus: 5th-6th c. BC Greek philosopher

Heraclius: 6th-7th c. Byzantine emperor

Heraiscus: Hellenistic hieroglyphical writer

Hercules: Graeco-Roman mythological hero, the son of Zeus

Hermes Trismegistus: the (legendary) mystical Egyptian writer whose reputed works form the corpus of Hermetic philosophy

Herodotus: 5th c. BC Greek historian

Hevelius: 17th c. German astronomer

Hippocrates: 5th-4th c. BC Greek doctor, and father of medicine; another Hippocrates was a 5th c. BC Greek geometer

Hofmannus: 17th c. German doctor and medical writer

Horus Apollo: *see* Orus Apollo

Isidore: 6th-7th c. Sevillian saint, archbishop and scholar

Jair: a judge of Israel (Judges 10:3-5) who was buried in Canaan

Jerome: 4th-5th c. saint and Latin Father of the Church; translator of the Greek Bible into Latin (the 'Vulgate')

Johnstonus: 17th c. Scottish naturalist

Josephus: 1st c. Jewish historian

Joubertus: 16th c. French encyclopaedist

Julia: niece of Domitian, with whom he carried on an adulterous relationship, and who died as a result of the abortifacient she was given by him.

Julian 'the Apostate': 4th c. Eastern Roman emperor who denied
  Christianity
Junius: 'the Elder', 16th c. French Protestant theologian
Justin: early 6th c. Eastern Roman emperor
Justinianus: early 6th c. Eastern Roman emperor

Kelley: John Dee's dishonest assistant in alchemical projects
Kiranides: a medieval collection of writings originally Arabic which
  were transmitted *via* Greek. The Arabic root of 'kiranides' means
  'collection'
Kircherus: 17th c. German Jesuit, priest, and scientist, author of more
  than forty scientific books

Lampridius: 4th c. Roman historian
LeGros: a friend and the son of a patient of Browne's of Crostwick
  Hall, near Norwich
Leo Africanus: 15th-16th c. Arab travel writer
Licinus: 4th c. Roman emperor
Linschoten: 16th-17th c. Dutch traveller and explorer
Love, Dr: Warden of Winchester during Browne's schooldays there
Lucan: 1st c. Roman epic poet of the war between Pompey and Caesar
Lucina: the goddess of childbirth
Lucretius: 1st c. BC Latin poet and Epicurean philosopher
Lusitanus: 16th c. Portuguese medic, botanical and anatomical writer
Luther: 15th-16th c. German priest and scholar whose writings re-
  marks instigated in 1519 the first official break from Rome in the
  Reformation
Lycurgus: mythical Spartan law-maker

Macrobius: 4th-5th c. Roman philosopher and grammarian
Maecenas: friend of Emperor Augustus and aristocratic patron of Vergil
Marcellus: 3rd c. BC Roman consul and general who fell in battle
  against Hannibal in southern Italy
Marius: 2nd-1st c. BC Roman general
Marlianus: 16th c. Italian antiquarian
Mathiolus: 16th c. Italian medic and botanist
Matilda: or Maud, 12th c. queen and empress of England
Mausolus: 4th c. BC king of Caria
Menoeceus: a Theban hero whose funeral pyre is described by Statius
Methuselah: Biblical figure known only for having lived the longest of
  all men (969 years)

Mercurio, Scipio: 16th-17th c. Italian encyclopaedist
Merrett: 17th c. English naturalist
Michaelangelo: 15th-16th c. Italian painter, sculptor, and architect
Mithridates: 1st c. BC king of Pontus
Moloch: a pagan god of the Phoenicians
Mopsus: a mythological participant in the Trojan War who, with
    Amphilocus, later shared an oracle shrine in Cilicia in Asia Minor
Morpheus: the god of dreams
Morta: *see* Atropus

Nebuchadnezzar: 7th-6th c. BC king of Babylon
Nicander: 3rd-2nd c. BC Greek writer on pharmacology and natural
    history
Nierembergius: 17th c. Spanish mystic, theologian, and occult writer
Numa: the mythical second king of Rome

Olaus: 15th-16th c. Swedish historian
Orus: Horus, or Harpocrates, Egyptian god variously identified with
    the sun, the sky, and vengeance, son of Isis and Osiris
Orus Apollo Niliacus: Horus Apollo or Horapollo, 5th c. Egyptian
    Greek author of *Hieroglyphica*, a book of apparently Egyptian sym-
    bols and thought by the Renaissance to be the key to Egyptian
    priestly wisdom. The manuscript, discovered at Andros in 1415
    and published 1505, was directly responsible for the ensuing cen-
    tury-long fashion for emblems and other symbolical pictures
Ortelius: 16th c. Flemish cartographer and engraver
Osiris: Egyptian god of fertility and burial

Palaephatus: 4th c. BC Greek commentator on mythology
Pan: Greek nature god, half man, half goat
Pancirollus: 16th-17th c. Italian antiquarian
Paracelsus: 15th-16th c. German physician and alchemist who estab-
    lished chemistry as a part of medicine
Pareus: 16th-17th c. German philologist and divine
Patroclus: Greek warrior at Troy whose death Achilles mourned ob-
    sessively
Penelope: wife of Ulysses who fended off suitors for three years until
    her husband returned from his adventures
Pererius: a 16th c. Spanish commentator on Genesis
Periander: 7th-6th c. BC Greek statesman
Pharamond: mythical first king of France

Philippus: 1st c. Roman rhetor and collector of the Garland of Philip, a part of the *Greek Anthology*

Philopoemen: 3rd-2nd c. BC Greek military leader

Philostratus (the Younger): 2nd c. Latin-Greek author who discusses real or imaginary paintings on mythical subjects

Philostratus the Elder: 2nd c. Latin biographer of Apollonius

Phocylides: 6th c. BC Greek philosopher and poet

Pierius: 15th-16th c. Italian scholar and emblem-writer

Pilate: Roman governor of Judea who condemned Christ to execution

Pinto: 16th c. Portuguese adventurer and travel writer

Plato: 5th-4th c. BC Greek philosopher

Platonism: philosophy based on the writings of Plato, which postulates an unchanging and eternal realm of realities independent of the sensory world

Pliny: the Elder, 1st c. Roman natural historian

Plutarch: 1st-2nd c. Greek biographer

Polydorus: Polydore Vergil, 16th c. Italian historian of early Britain

Pompey: 2nd-1st c. BC Roman general

Poppaea: the Jewish wife of Nero, 1st c. Roman emperor

Porta: see Della Porta

Posthumus: 3rd c. Gallic emperor

Primerose: 17th c. English medical writer

Priscian: an early 6th c. Latin grammarian

Procopius: 6th c. Byzantine historian of the reigns of Justin and Justinian

Propertius: 1st c. BC Roman poet

Psellus: 11th c. Byzantine philosopher and theologian

Purchas: 16th-17th c. English collector of travel writing

Pyrrhus: 4th-3rd c. BC king of Epirus and military theorist

Pythagoras: 6th c. BC philospher and mathematician, and founder of the school of thought bearing his name which studied numerology and other patterns in nature, and believed in the transmigration of souls

Raphael: 15th-16th c. Italian painter and architect

Ray, John: English naturalist and zoologist

Regiomontanus: 15th c. inventor Johan Muller of Königsberg

Rhodiginus: 15th-16th c. Italian scholar

Ringo: 8th c. king of Sweden

Rondeletius: 16th c. French naturalist

Royal Society: The Royal Society of London for the Promotion of

Natural Knowledge, one of the oldest scientific societies in Europe, founded 1660 largely by Baconians. Early members included Newton, Wren, Glanvill, Hooke, Dryden, and Halley

Rudolphus: the Holy Roman Emperor of the 16th-17th c.

Sabellicus: 16th c. Italian classical scholar and philologist

de Salignaco, Bartholomeus: 16th c. writer on Jerusalem

Sammonicus: 2nd-3rd c. Roman author of a book on natural curiosities

Saloninus: son of Galienus

Sanctius: commentator on Alciati, the first and most famous emblematist, in a book of 1573

Sardanapalus: 9th c. BC king of Assyria

Saxo: 12th-13th c. Danish historian

Scaliger: 'the Younger', 16th c. French scholar

Scaliger: 'the Elder', 16th c.Italian scholar and philosopher

Septuagint: the oldest and most important form of the Old Testament, translated from Hebrew and Aramaic into Greek in the centuries before the birth of Christ

Sertorius: 1st c. BC Roman commander

Severus: any of three so-named Roman emperors in the 1st-4th c.

Sigonius: 16th c. Italian historian and Greek scholar

Snilling, Ulfketel: led the East Anglian forces against Sweyn in 1004

Solinus: 3rd c. Latin geographer and encyclopaedist

Somnus: the god of dreams

Starkatterus: legendary hero described by Saxo Grammaticus

Stoics: philosophy of indifference to all but virtue and moral weakness; the Stoics believed that true happiness comes only from virtue

Strabo: Roman geographer and military historian at the time of Christ who discussed the British Isles under the Romans

Sueno/Sweyn: 10th-11th c. king of Denmark who conquered England;

Sylla: 2nd c. BC Roman general

Syrach, son of: Ben-Sira, author of the apocryphal Biblical book 'The Wisdom of Ben-Sira' or 'Sirach' for short

Tacitus: 1st c. Roman historian

Tamerlane: Tamberlaine, the 14th c. central Asian warlord who conquered states from Mongolia to the Mediterranean.

Tertullian: 2nd-3rd c. Latin father of the church

Tetricus: 3rd c. Gallic Roman emperor

Thales: 6th c. BC Greek philosopher

Themison: 1st c. Greek medical writer and fashionable but fraudulent doctor in Rome

Themistocles: 5th c. BC Greek general responsible for defeating the Persians at Salamis

Theodosius: 5th c. Byzantine emperor

Thersites: a foul-tongued railer among the Greeks at Troy

Tiberius: 1st c. Roman emperor

Tiresias: a Theban soothsayer

Titus: 1st c. Roman emperor

Trajan: 1st-2nd c. Roman emperor

Tremellius: 16th c. Italian Hebrew scholar

Unguinus: 8th c. Swedish king

Urbin: Raphael of Urbino

Valens: 4th c. Eastern Roman emperor

Vergil: 1st c. BC Roman poet

Vespasian: 1st c. Roman emperor

Victorinus: 3rd c. Roman Gallic emperor

Vossius: 17th c. Dutch Pythagorean and historian of philosophy

Vulcan: or Hephaestus, god of fire and the smithy

William the Conqueror: Norman conqueror of England in 1066

Willughby: English ornithologist

Wormius: 16th-17th c. Danish antiquarian

Xerxes: 5th c. BC Persian victor over the Greeks at Thermopylae

Zeno: 4th-3rd c. BC Phoenician/Greek founder of Stoicism